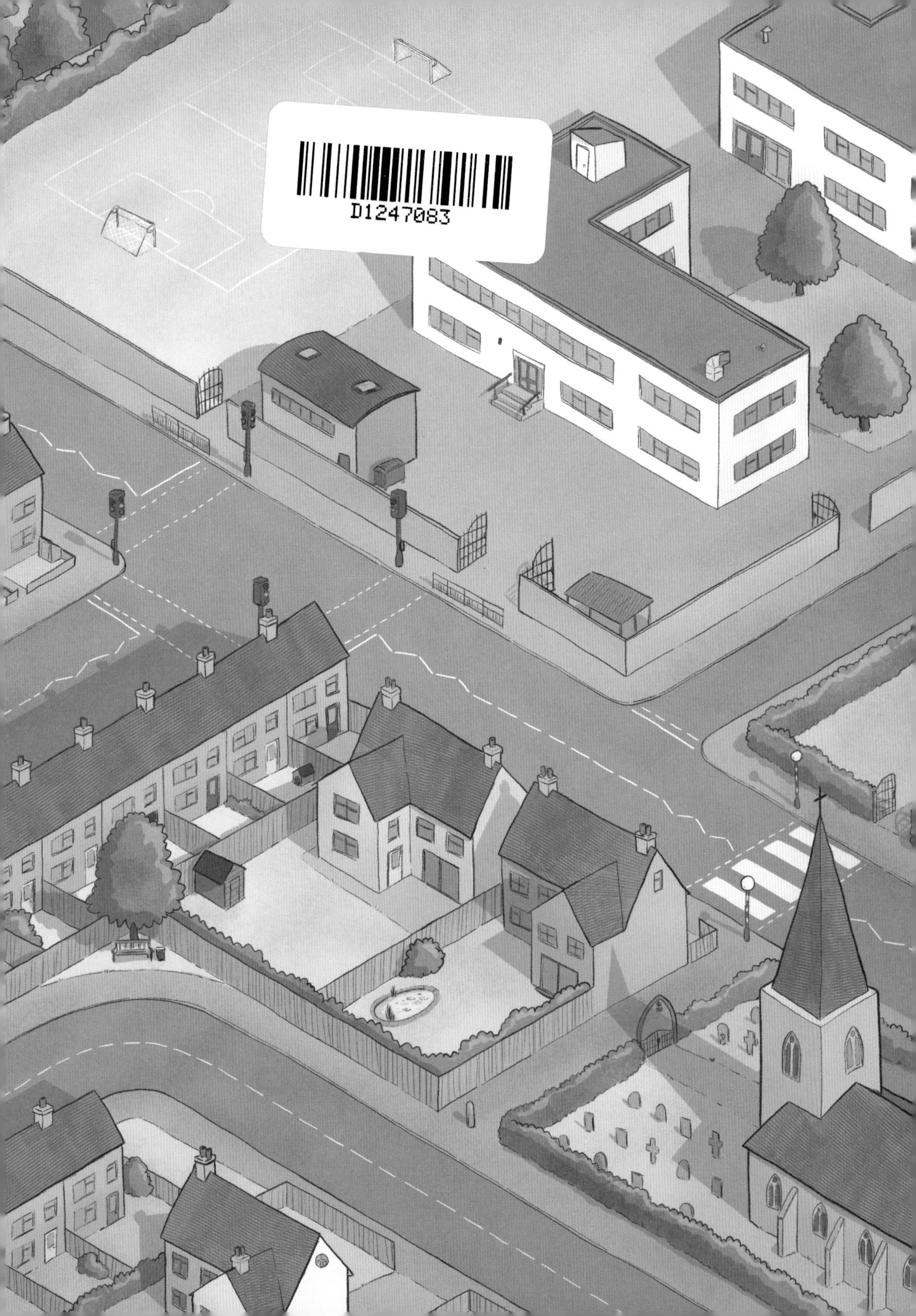

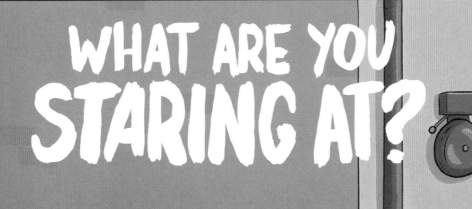

WHAT ARE YOU STARING AT?

MONDAYS WERE USUALLY JAKE'S BEST DAY OF THE WEEK.

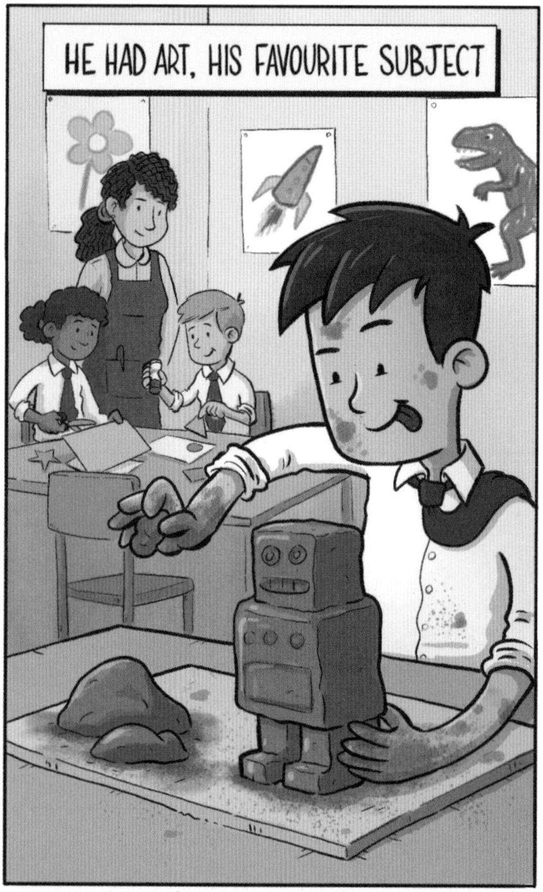
HE HAD ART, HIS FAVOURITE SUBJECT

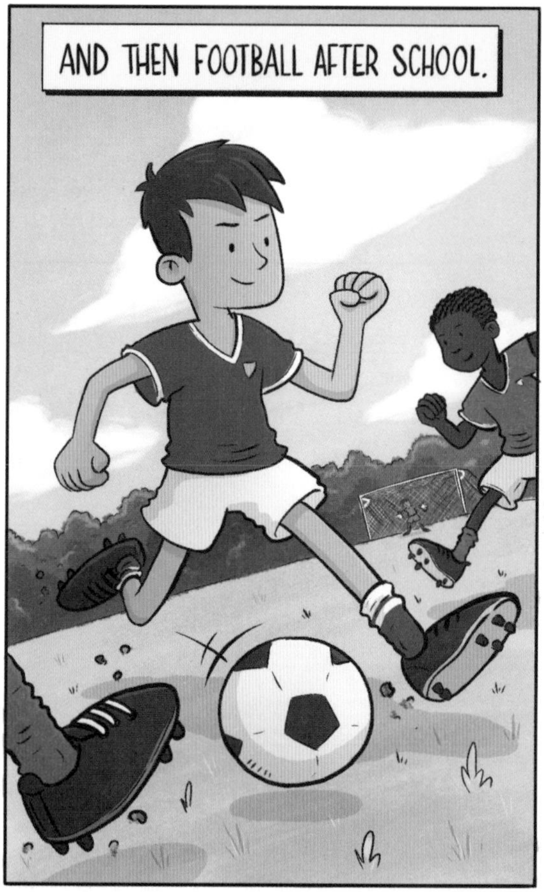
AND THEN FOOTBALL AFTER SCHOOL.

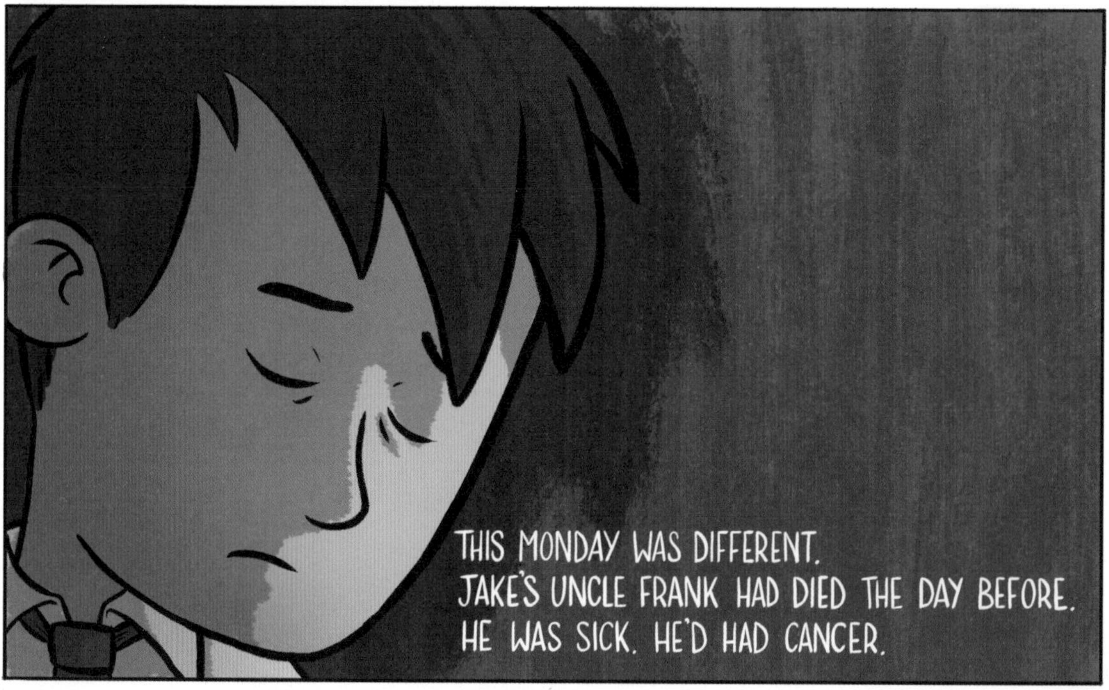
THIS MONDAY WAS DIFFERENT.
JAKE'S UNCLE FRANK HAD DIED THE DAY BEFORE.
HE WAS SICK. HE'D HAD CANCER.

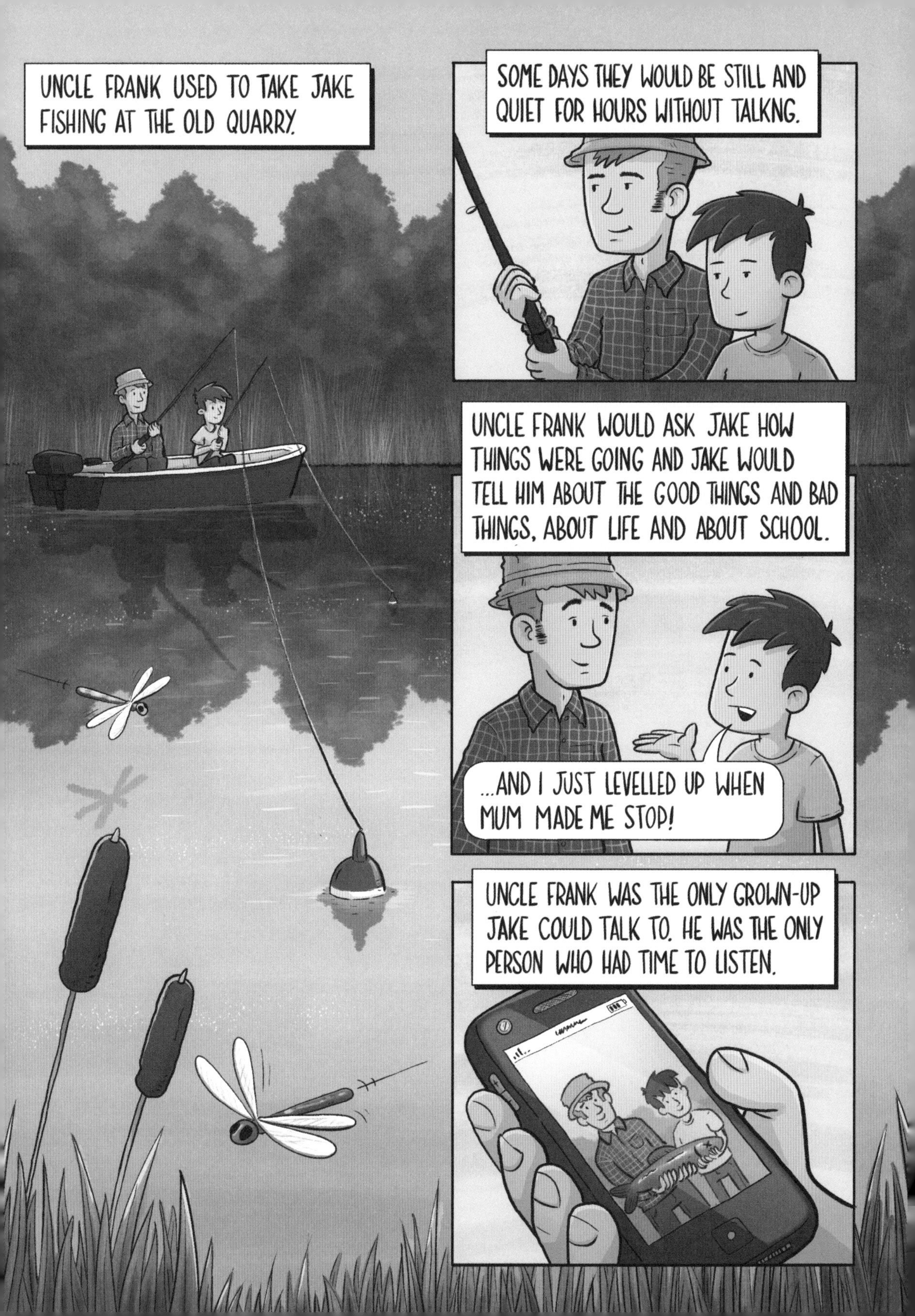
UNCLE FRANK USED TO TAKE JAKE FISHING AT THE OLD QUARRY.
SOME DAYS THEY WOULD BE STILL AND QUIET FOR HOURS WITHOUT TALKNG.
UNCLE FRANK WOULD ASK JAKE HOW THINGS WERE GOING AND JAKE WOULD TELL HIM ABOUT THE GOOD THINGS AND BAD THINGS, ABOUT LIFE AND ABOUT SCHOOL.
...AND I JUST LEVELLED UP WHEN MUM MADE ME STOP!
UNCLE FRANK WAS THE ONLY GROWN-UP JAKE COULD TALK TO. HE WAS THE ONLY PERSON WHO HAD TIME TO LISTEN.

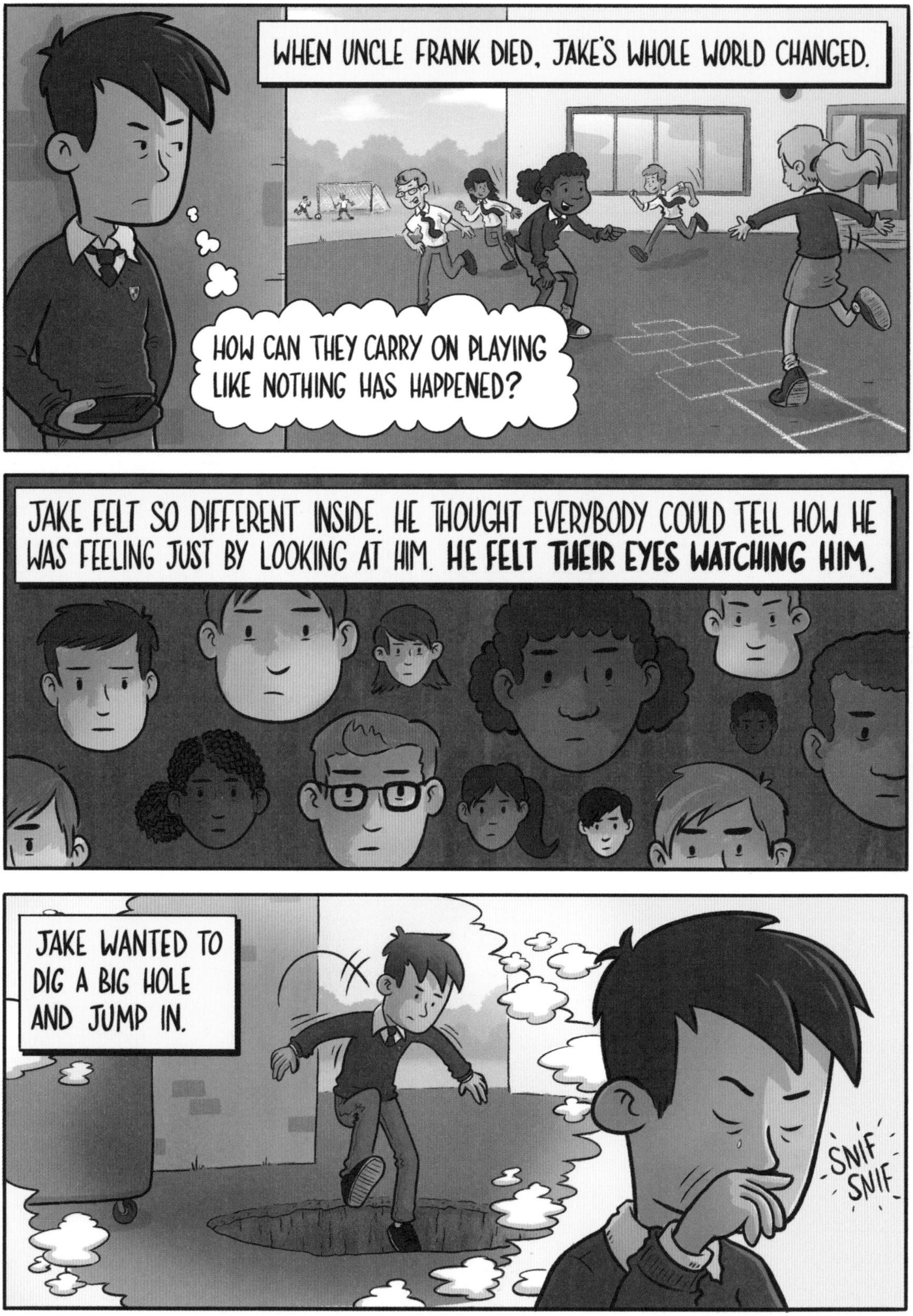
WHEN UNCLE FRANK DIED, JAKE'S WHOLE WORLD CHANGED.
HOW CAN THEY CARRY ON PLAYING LIKE NOTHING HAS HAPPENED?
JAKE FELT SO DIFFERENT INSIDE. HE THOUGHT EVERYBODY COULD TELL HOW HE WAS FEELING JUST BY LOOKING AT HIM. **HE FELT THEIR EYES WATCHING HIM.**
JAKE WANTED TO DIG A BIG HOLE AND JUMP IN.
SNIF SNIF

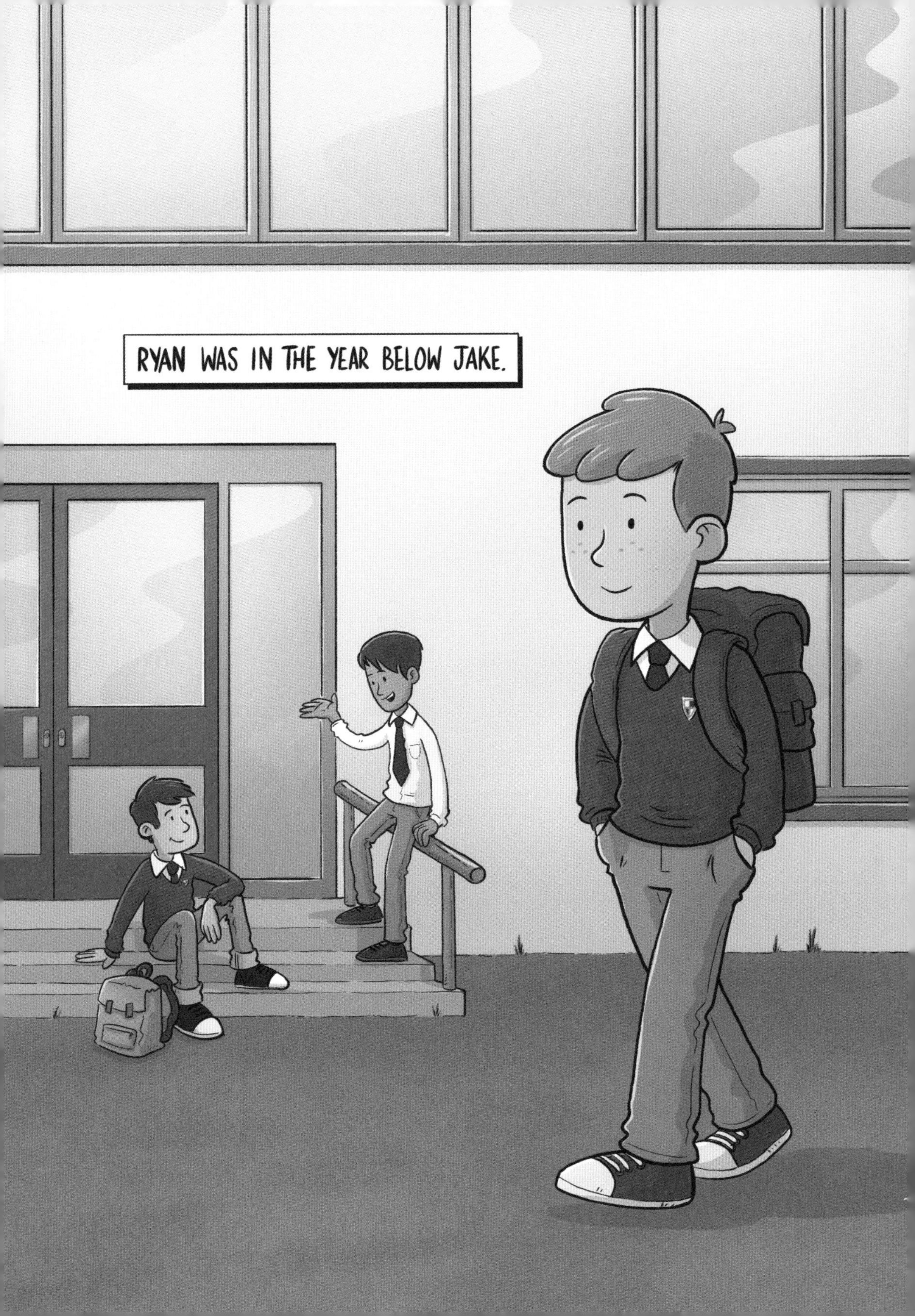
RYAN WAS IN THE YEAR BELOW JAKE.

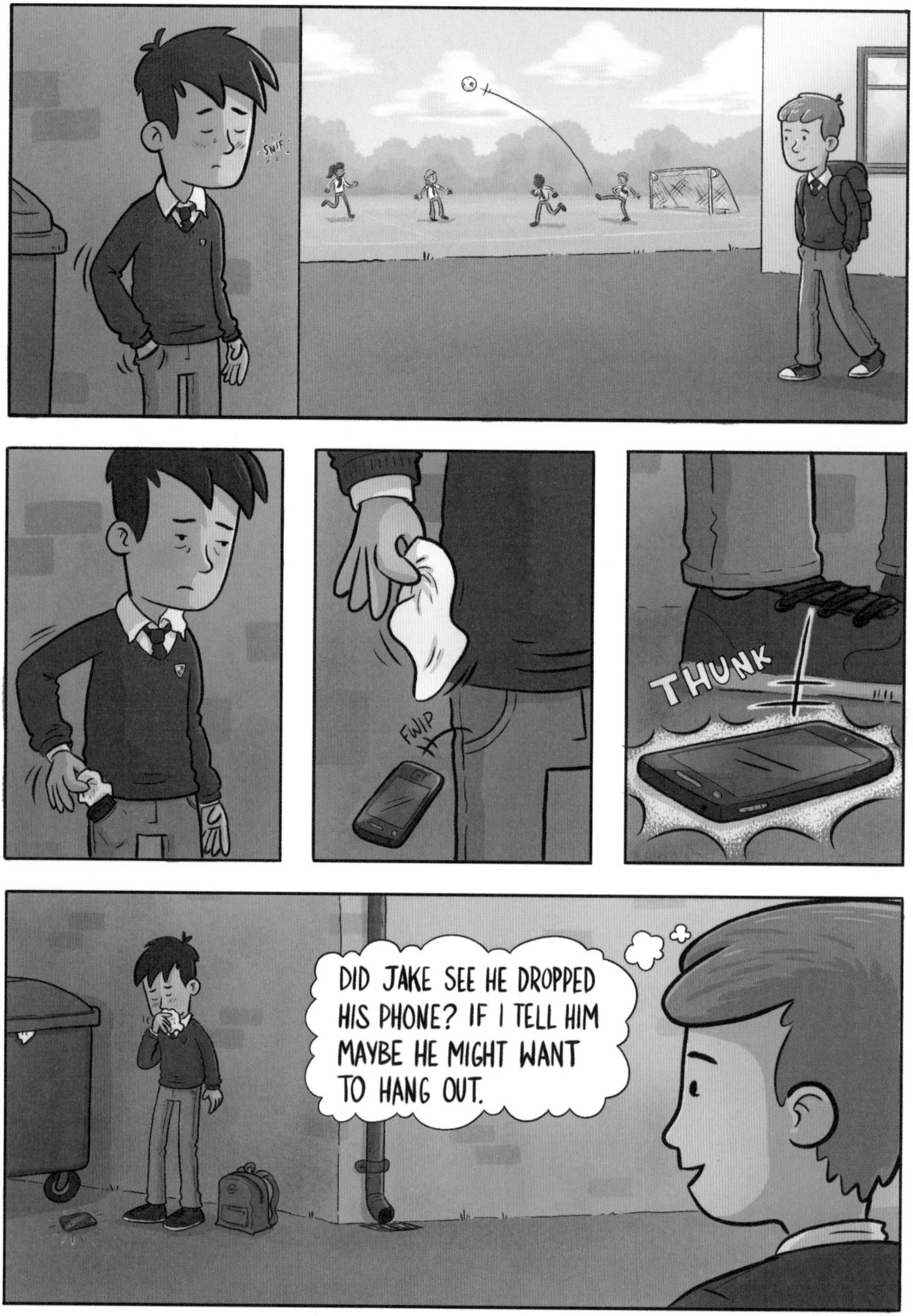
SNIF
FWIP
THUNK
DID JAKE SEE HE DROPPED HIS PHONE? IF I TELL HIM MAYBE HE MIGHT WANT TO HANG OUT.

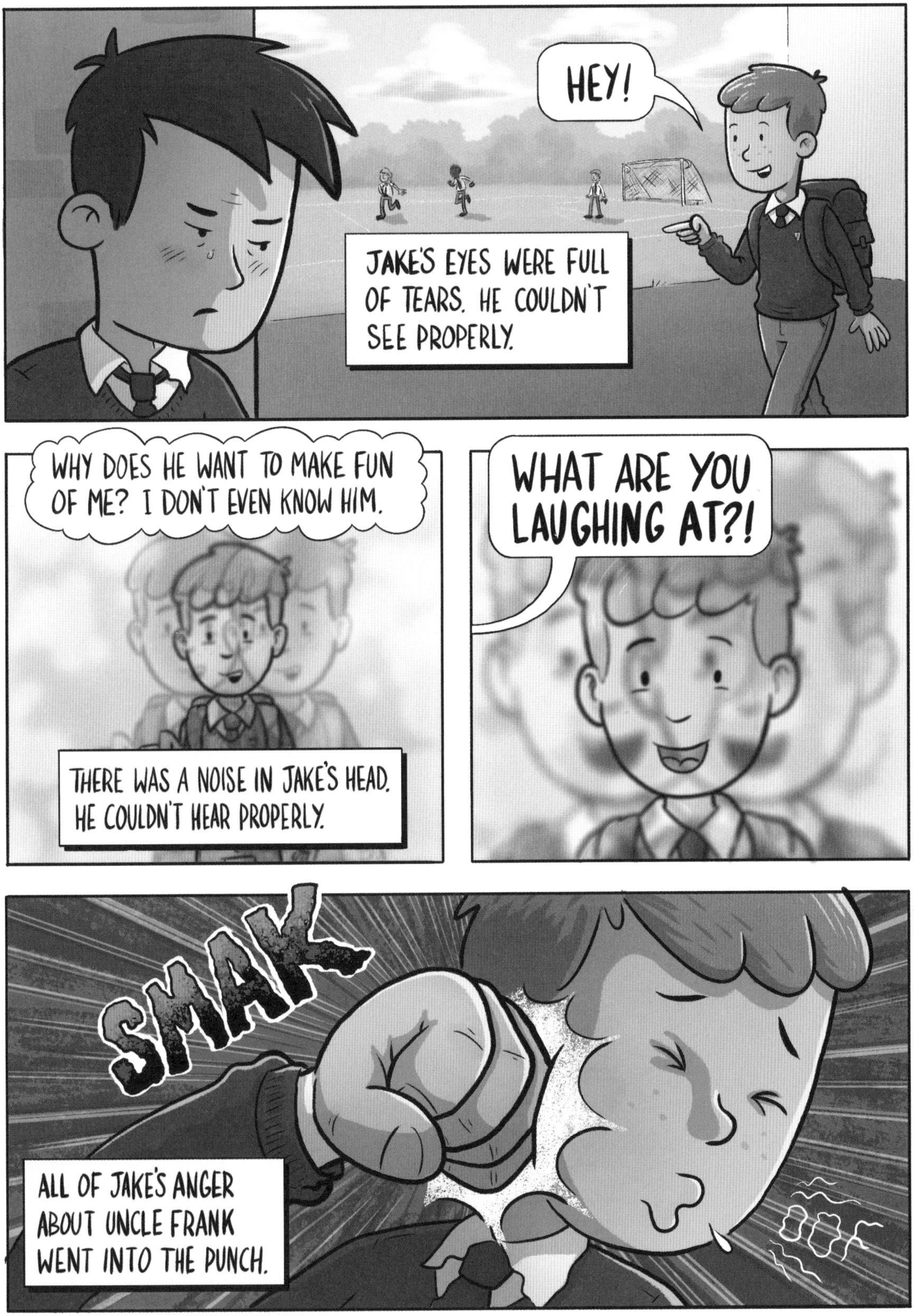
HEY!
JAKE'S EYES WERE FULL OF TEARS. HE COULDN'T SEE PROPERLY.
WHY DOES HE WANT TO MAKE FUN OF ME? I DON'T EVEN KNOW HIM.
THERE WAS A NOISE IN JAKE'S HEAD. HE COULDN'T HEAR PROPERLY.
WHAT ARE YOU LAUGHING AT?!
SMAK
ALL OF JAKE'S ANGER ABOUT UNCLE FRANK WENT INTO THE PUNCH.
OOF

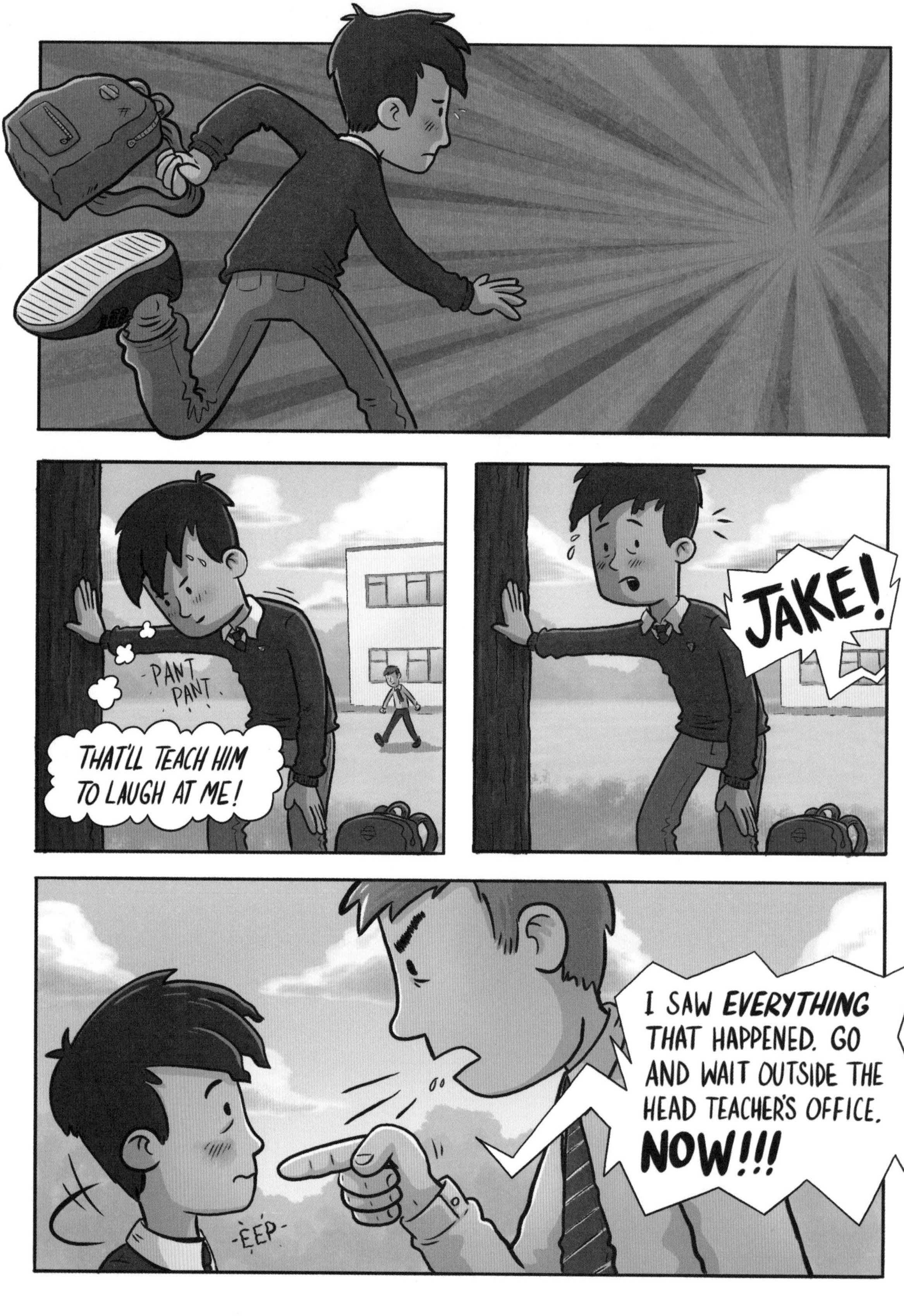
PANT PANT
THAT'LL TEACH HIM TO LAUGH AT ME!
JAKE!
I SAW EVERYTHING THAT HAPPENED. GO AND WAIT OUTSIDE THE HEAD TEACHER'S OFFICE. NOW!!!
EEP

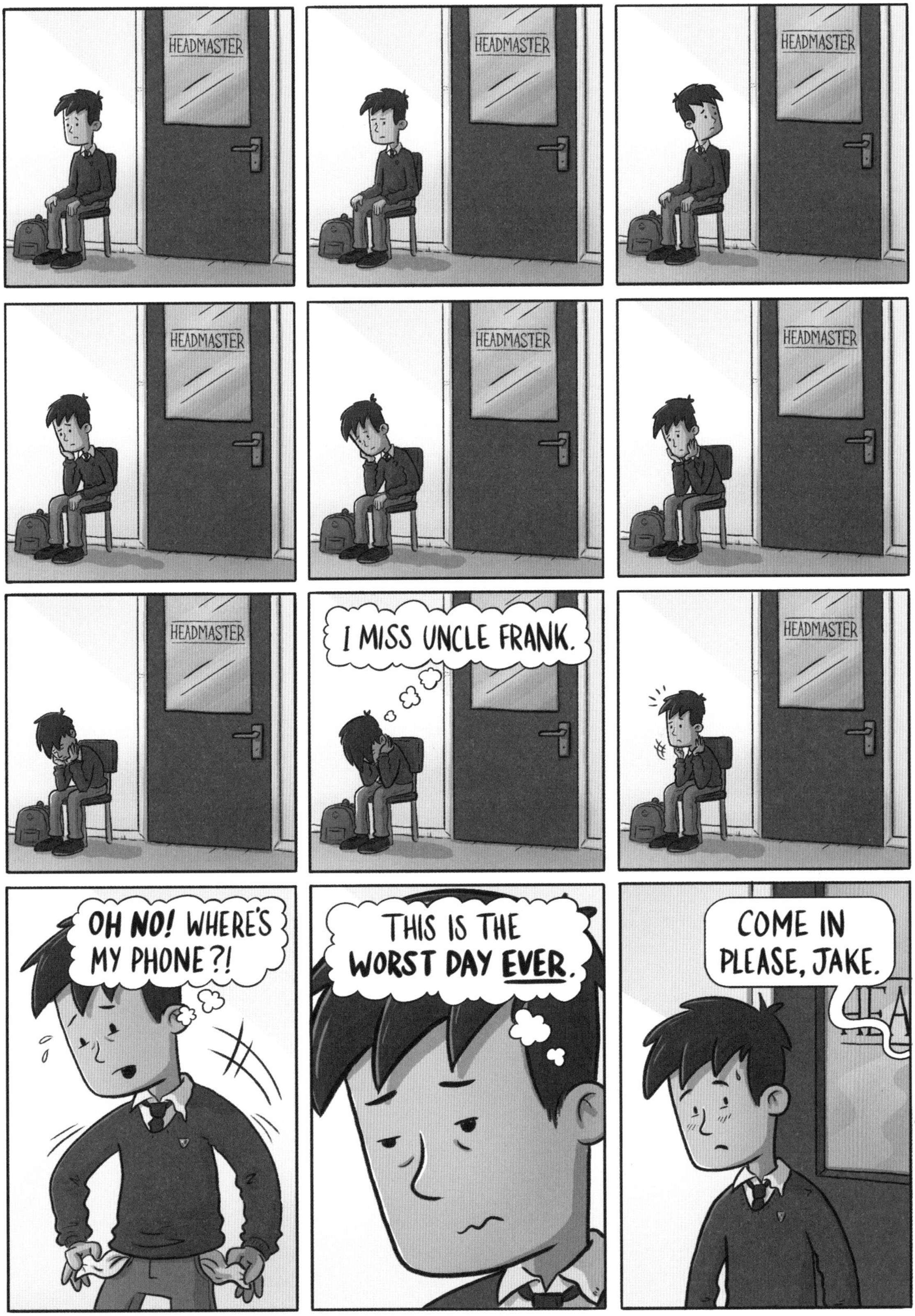
HEADMASTER
I MISS UNCLE FRANK.
OH NO! WHERE'S MY PHONE?!
THIS IS THE WORST DAY EVER.
COME IN PLEASE, JAKE.

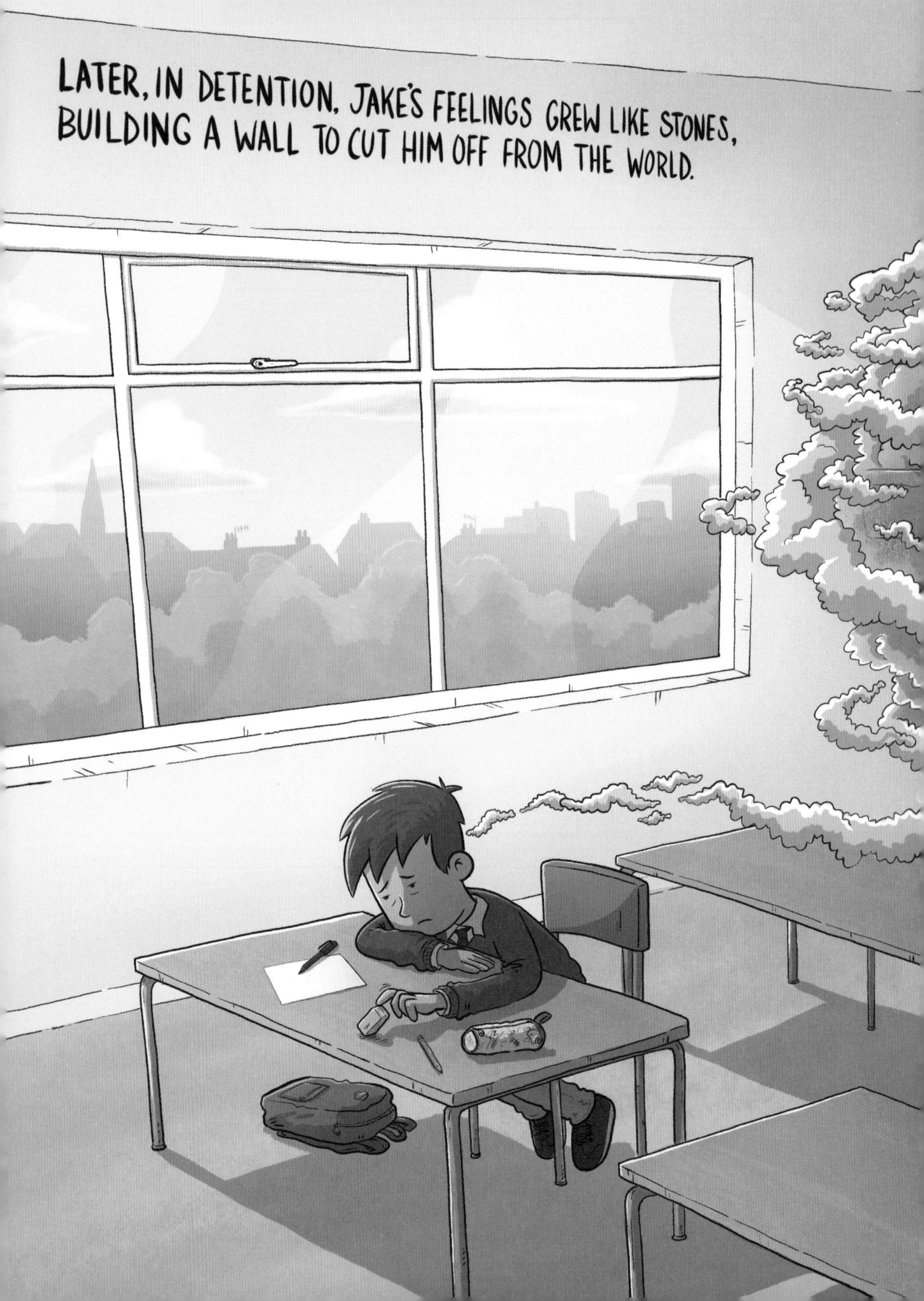
LATER, IN DETENTION, JAKE'S FEELINGS GREW LIKE STONES, BUILDING A WALL TO CUT HIM OFF FROM THE WORLD.

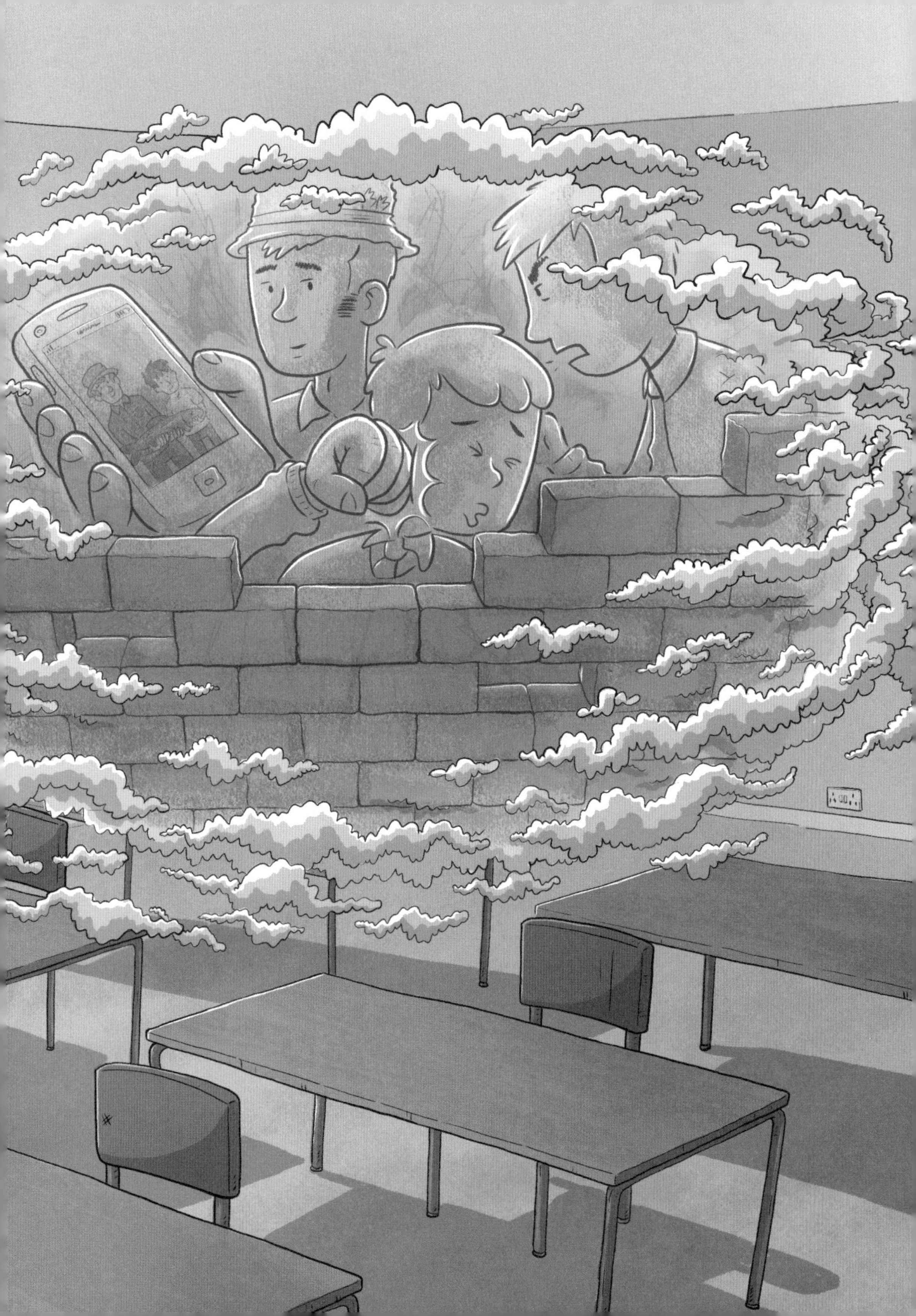

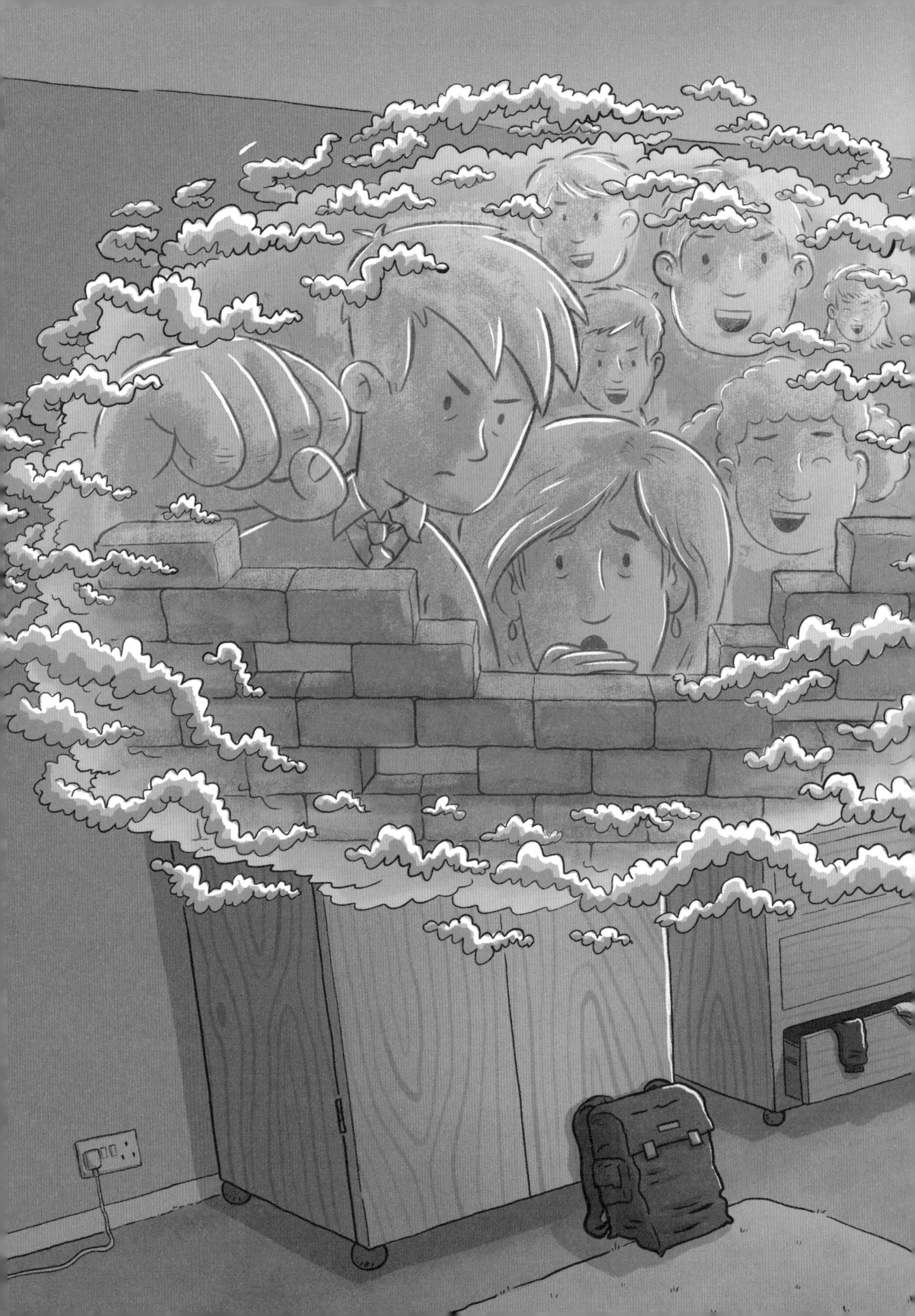

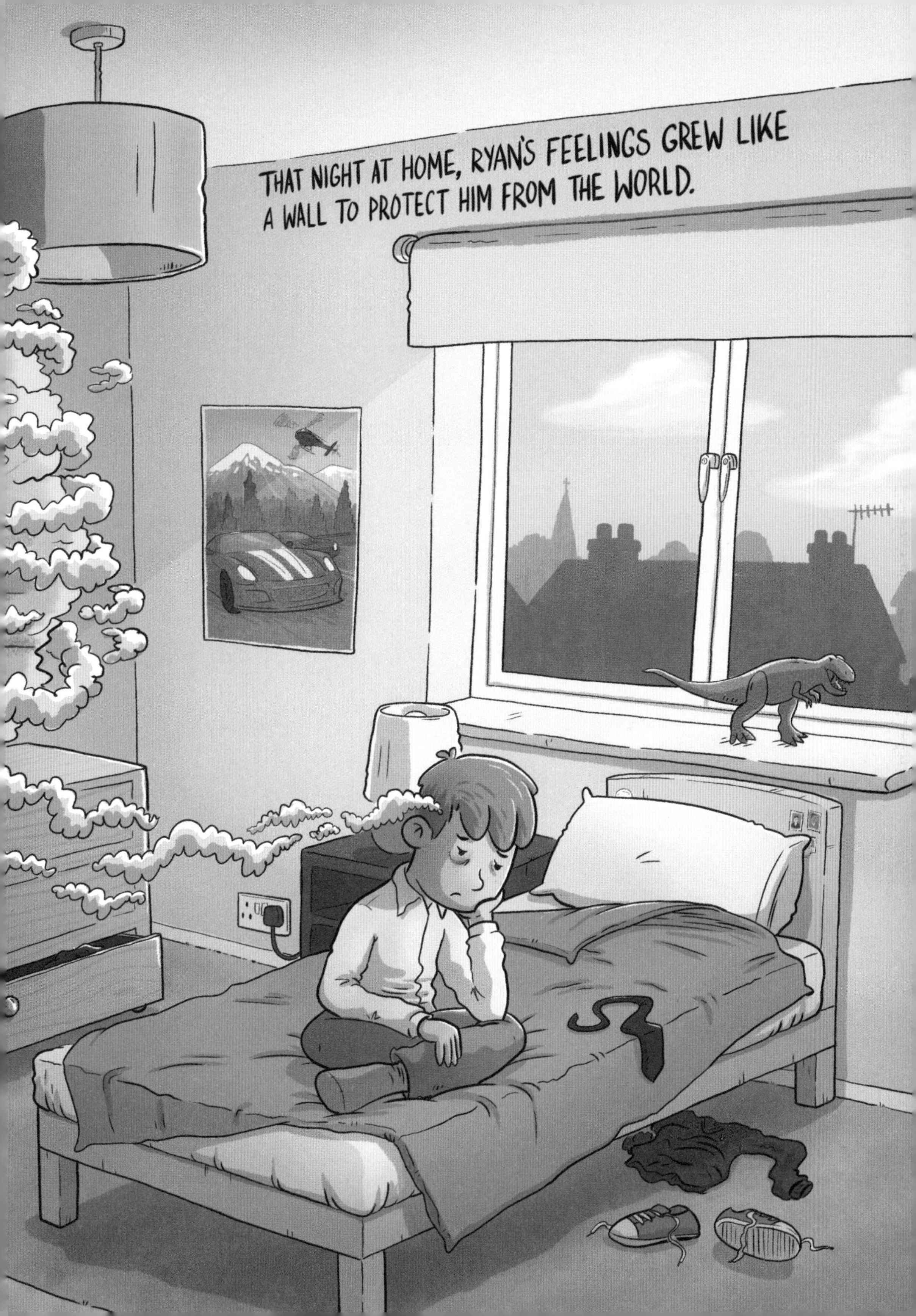
THAT NIGHT AT HOME, RYAN'S FEELINGS GREW LIKE A WALL TO PROTECT HIM FROM THE WORLD.

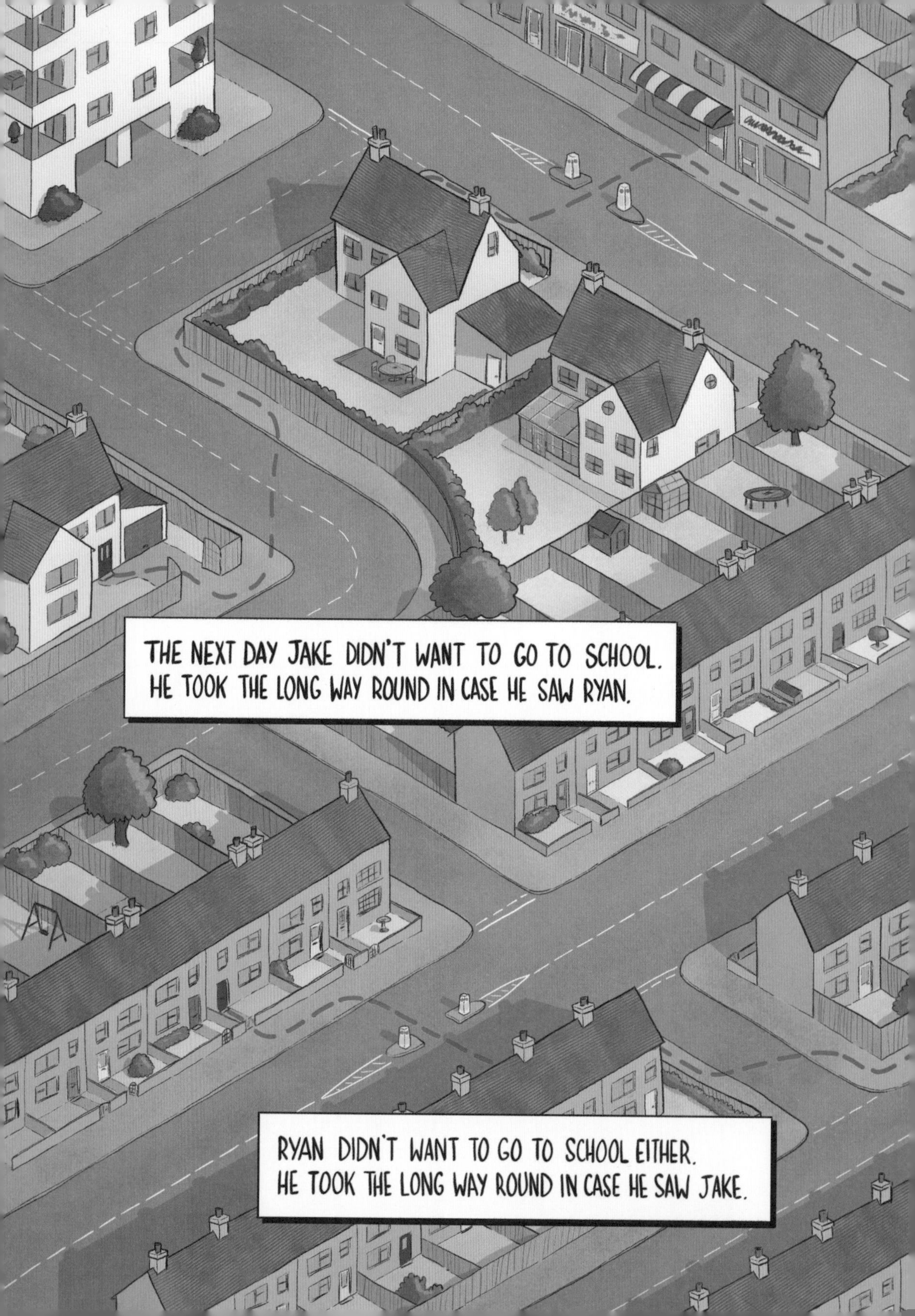
THE NEXT DAY JAKE DIDN'T WANT TO GO TO SCHOOL. HE TOOK THE LONG WAY ROUND IN CASE HE SAW RYAN.
RYAN DIDN'T WANT TO GO TO SCHOOL EITHER. HE TOOK THE LONG WAY ROUND IN CASE HE SAW JAKE.

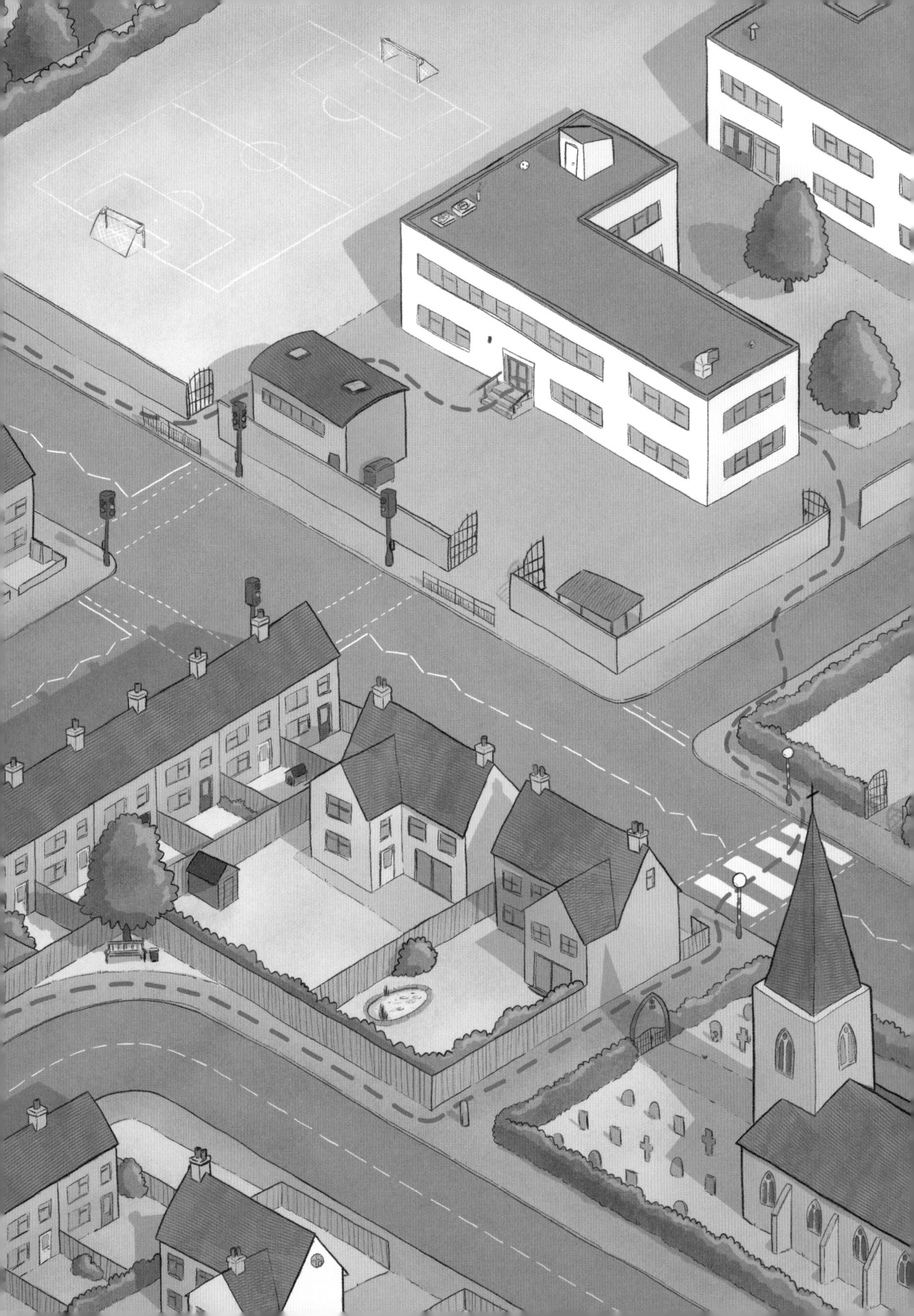

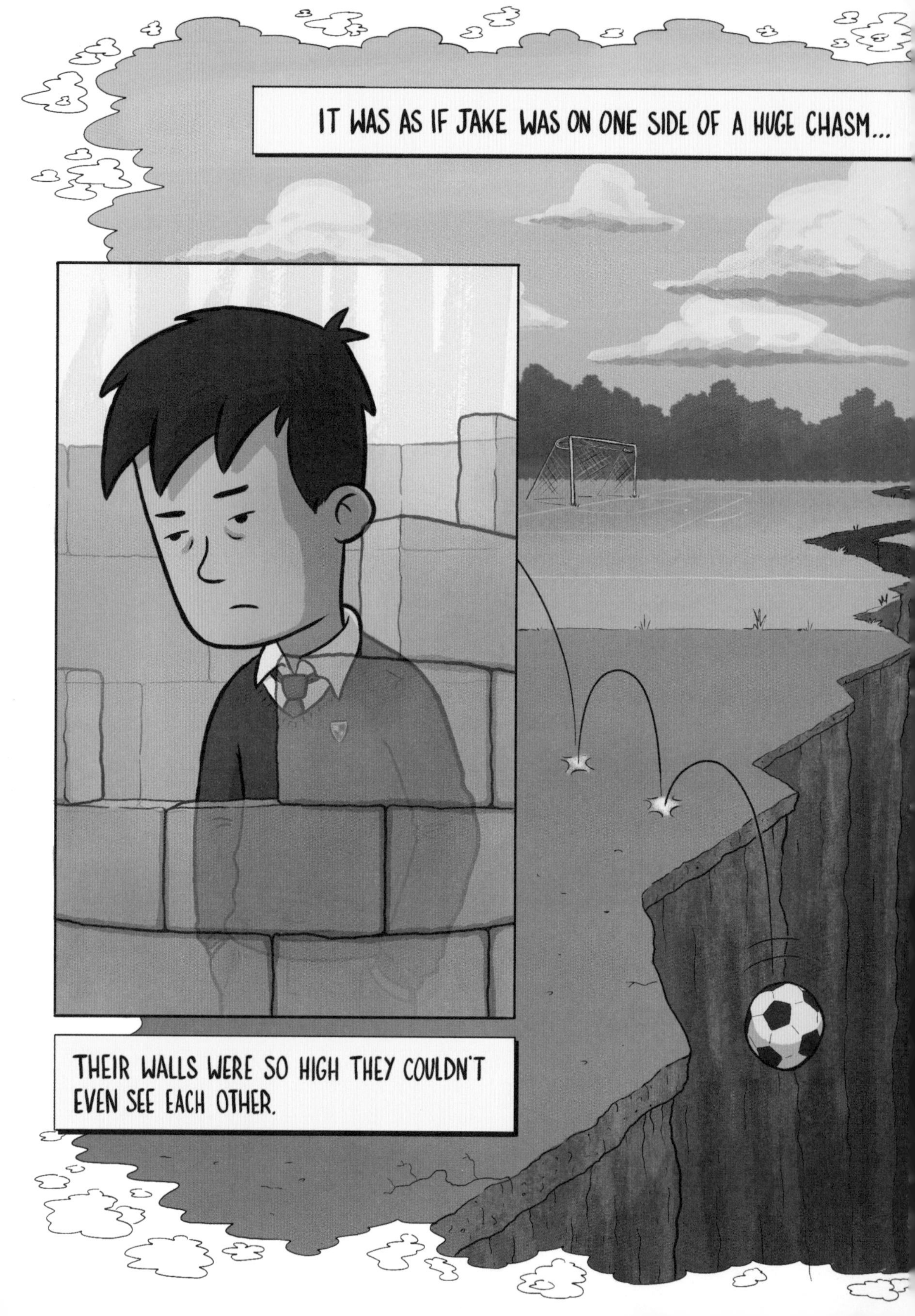
IT WAS AS IF JAKE WAS ON ONE SIDE OF A HUGE CHASM...
THEIR WALLS WERE SO HIGH THEY COULDN'T EVEN SEE EACH OTHER.

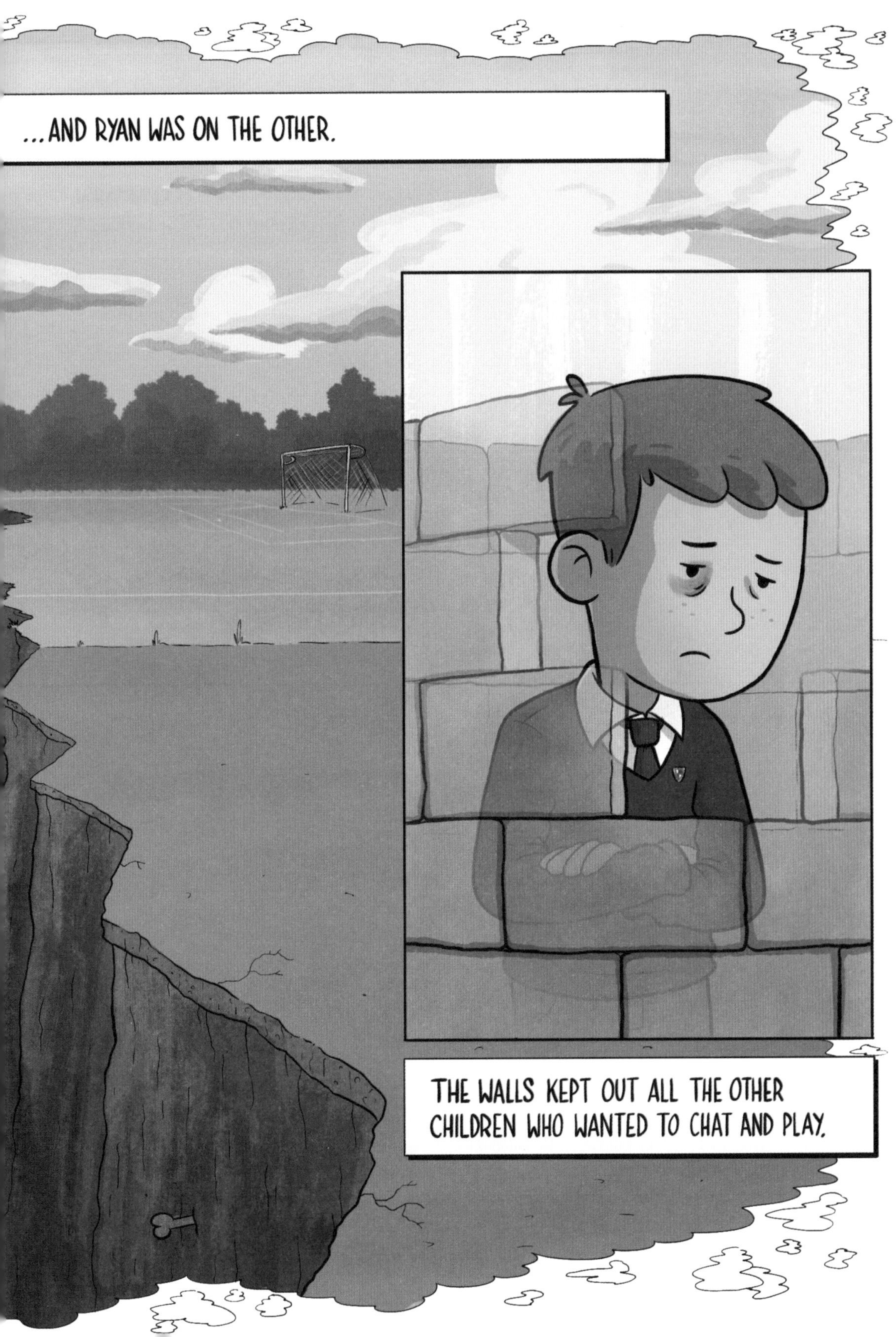
...AND RYAN WAS ON THE OTHER.
THE WALLS KEPT OUT ALL THE OTHER CHILDREN WHO WANTED TO CHAT AND PLAY.

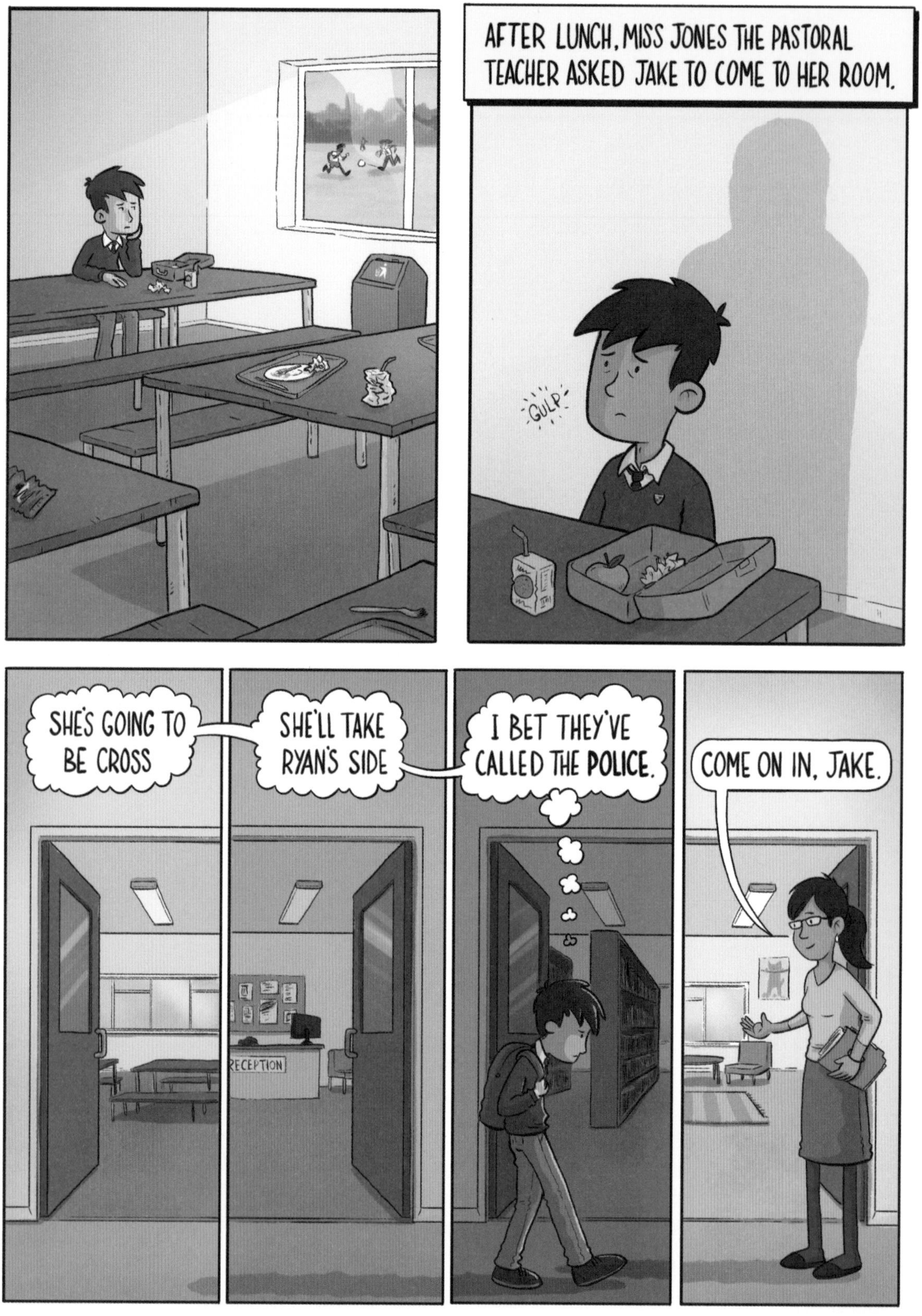
AFTER LUNCH, MISS JONES THE PASTORAL TEACHER ASKED JAKE TO COME TO HER ROOM.
GULP
SHE'S GOING TO BE CROSS
SHE'LL TAKE RYAN'S SIDE
I BET THEY'VE CALLED THE **POLICE**.
RECEPTION
COME ON IN, JAKE.

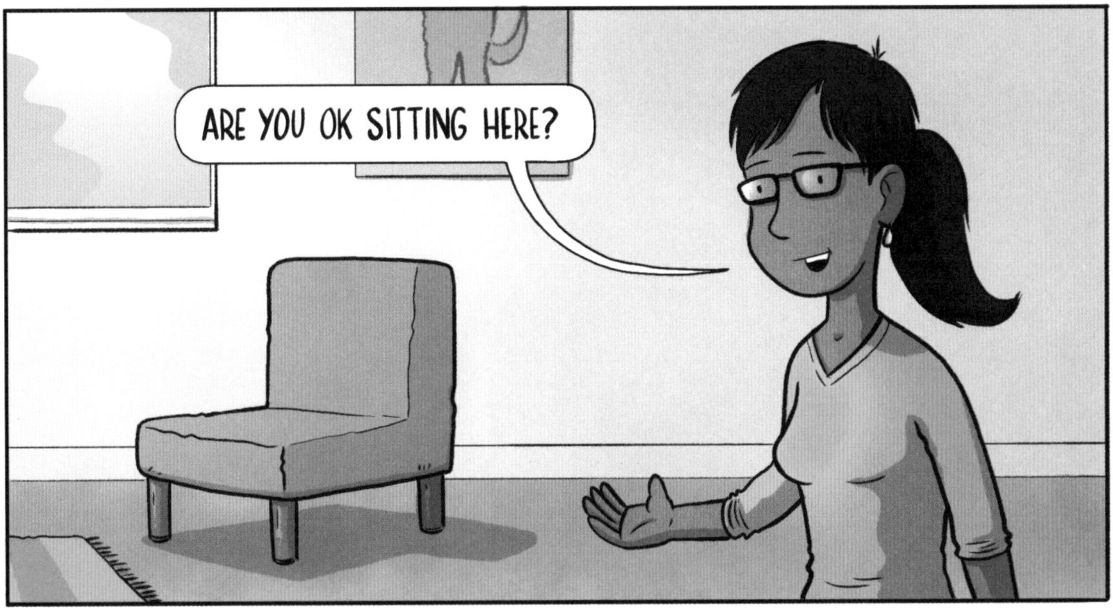
ARE YOU OK SITTING HERE?

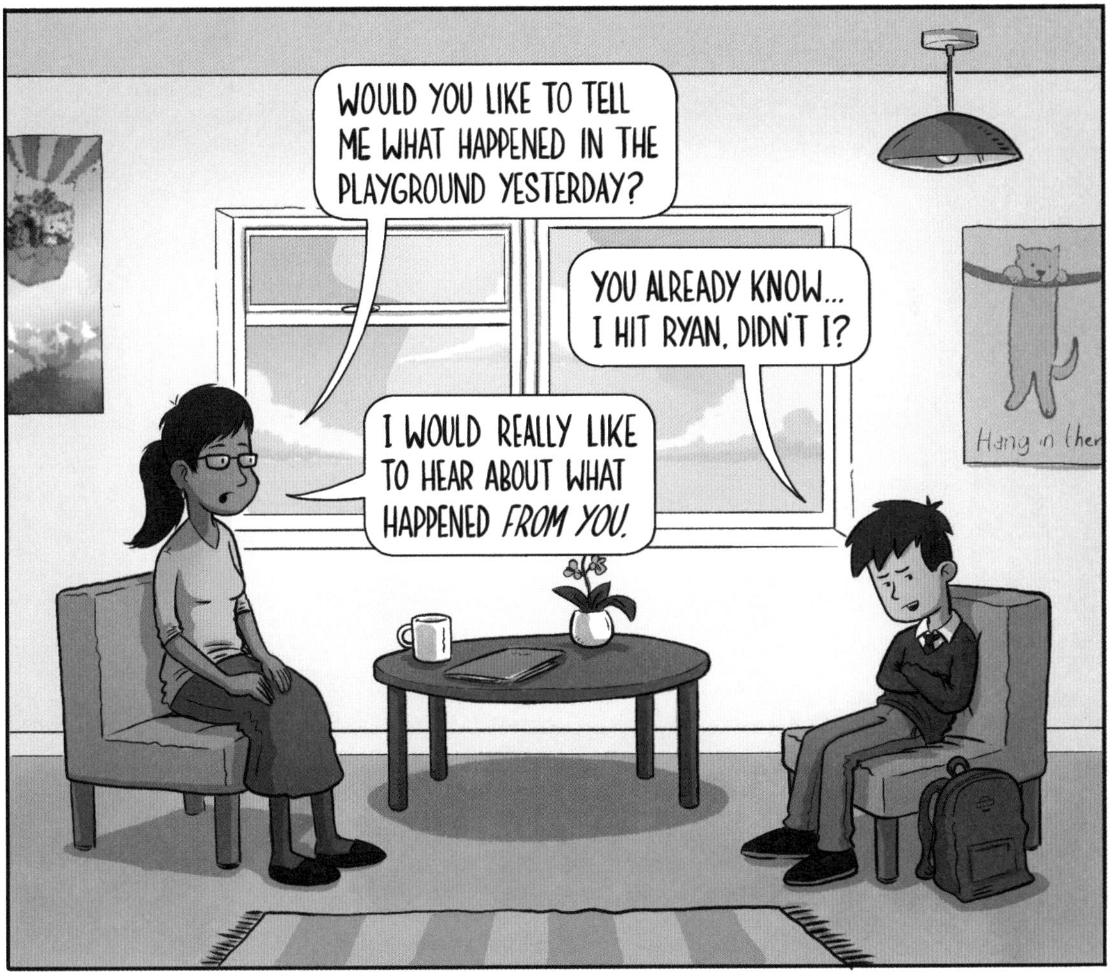
WOULD YOU LIKE TO TELL ME WHAT HAPPENED IN THE PLAYGROUND YESTERDAY?
YOU ALREADY KNOW... I HIT RYAN, DIDN'T I?
I WOULD REALLY LIKE TO HEAR ABOUT WHAT HAPPENED *FROM YOU.*
Hang in ther

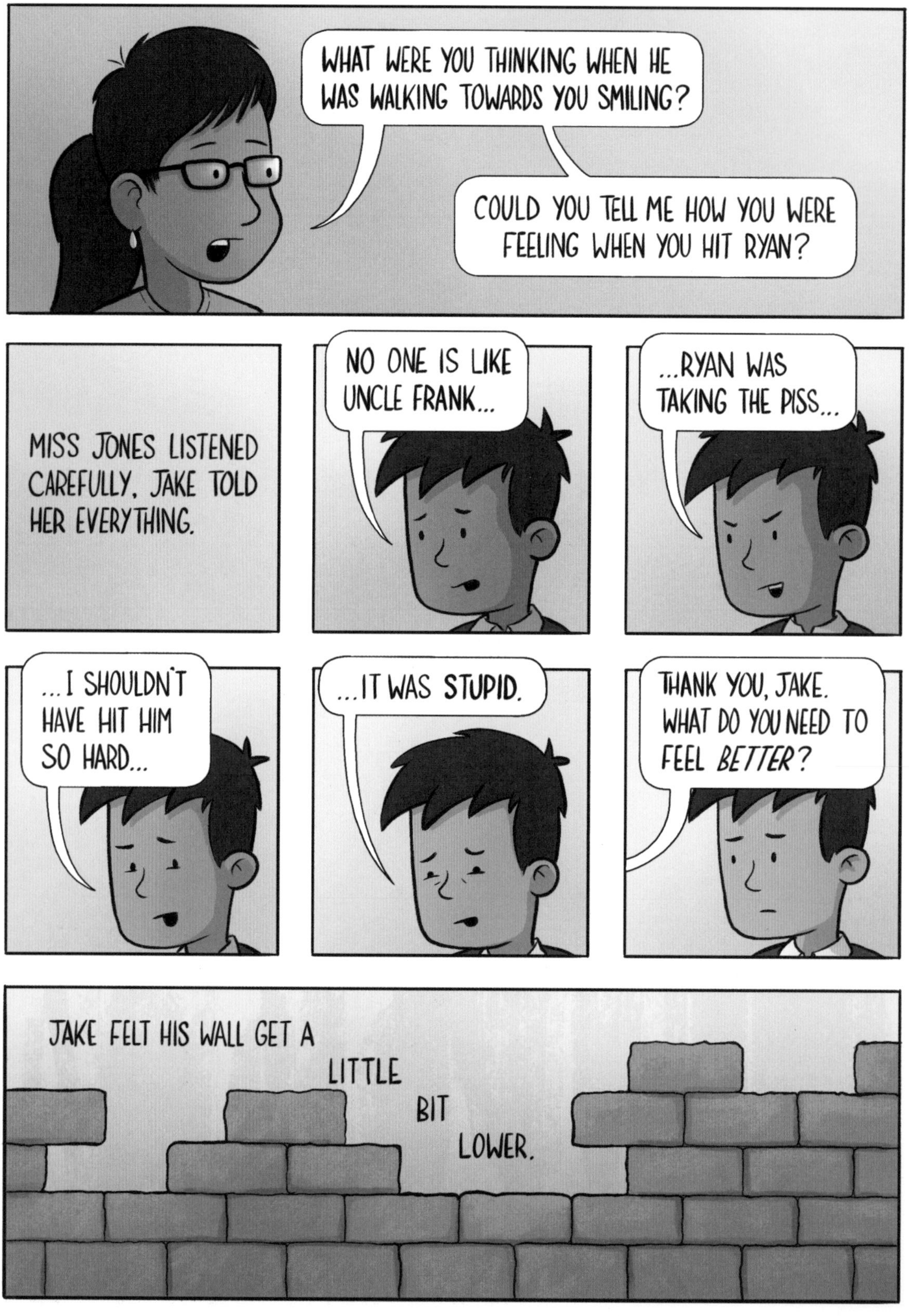
WHAT WERE YOU THINKING WHEN HE WAS WALKING TOWARDS YOU SMILING?
COULD YOU TELL ME HOW YOU WERE FEELING WHEN YOU HIT RYAN?
MISS JONES LISTENED CAREFULLY, JAKE TOLD HER EVERYTHING.
NO ONE IS LIKE UNCLE FRANK...
...RYAN WAS TAKING THE PISS...
...I SHOULDN'T HAVE HIT HIM SO HARD...
...IT WAS **STUPID.**
THANK YOU, JAKE. WHAT DO YOU NEED TO FEEL *BETTER*?
JAKE FELT HIS WALL GET A LITTLE BIT LOWER.

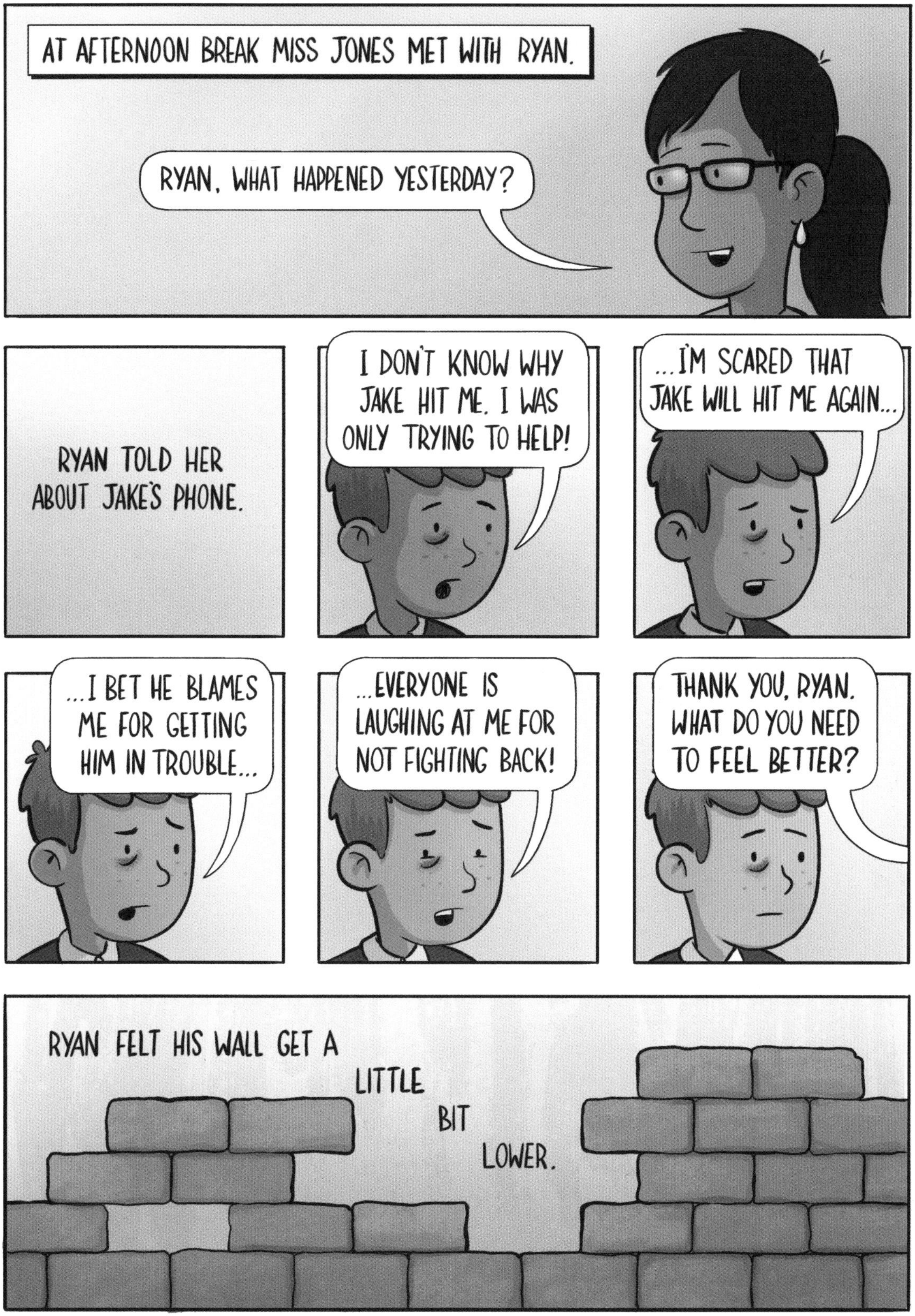
AT AFTERNOON BREAK MISS JONES MET WITH RYAN.
RYAN, WHAT HAPPENED YESTERDAY?
RYAN TOLD HER ABOUT JAKE'S PHONE.
I DON'T KNOW WHY JAKE HIT ME. I WAS ONLY TRYING TO HELP!
...I'M SCARED THAT JAKE WILL HIT ME AGAIN...
...I BET HE BLAMES ME FOR GETTING HIM IN TROUBLE...
...EVERYONE IS LAUGHING AT ME FOR NOT FIGHTING BACK!
THANK YOU, RYAN. WHAT DO YOU NEED TO FEEL BETTER?
RYAN FELT HIS WALL GET A LITTLE BIT LOWER.

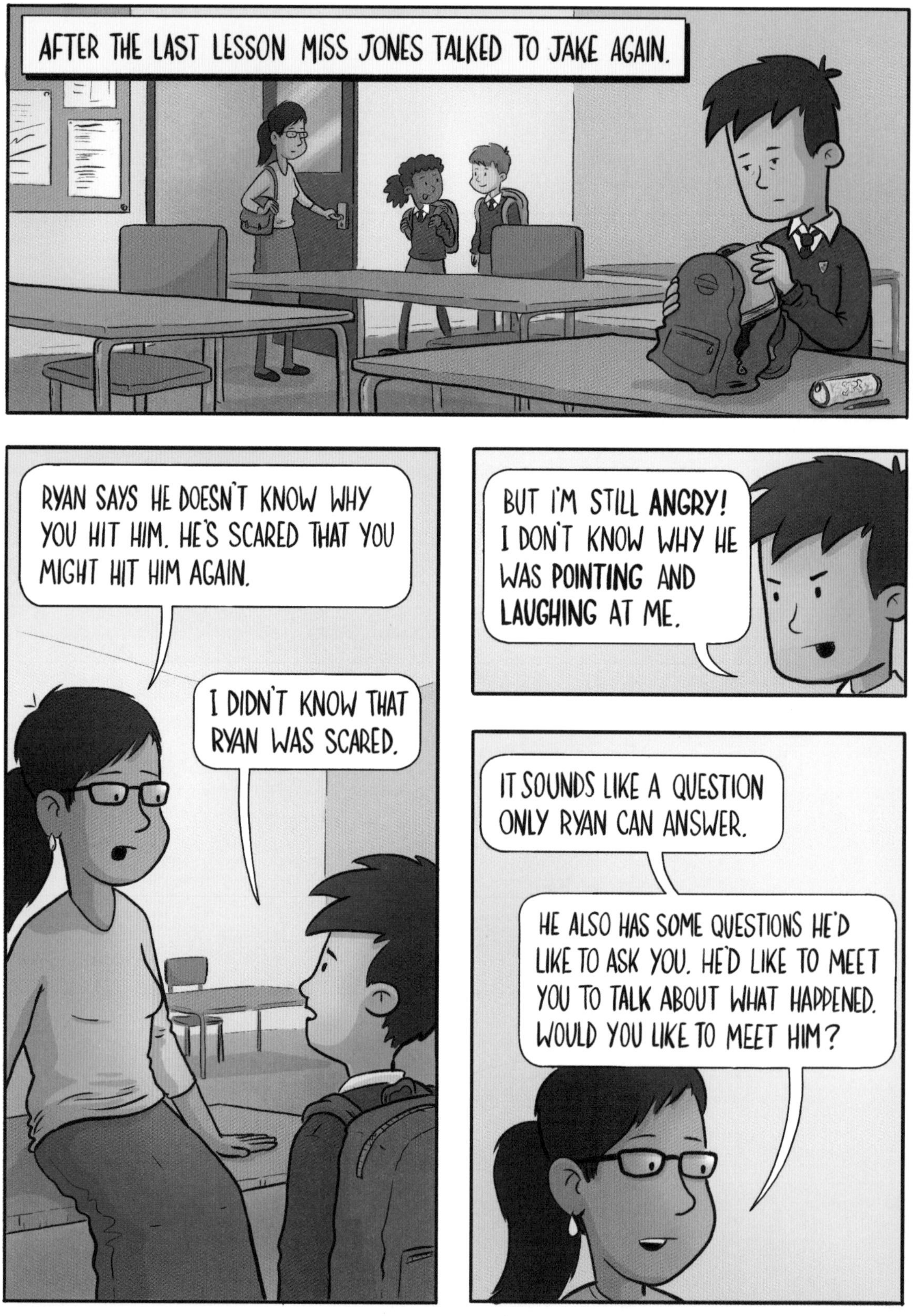
AFTER THE LAST LESSON MISS JONES TALKED TO JAKE AGAIN.
RYAN SAYS HE DOESN'T KNOW WHY YOU HIT HIM. HE'S SCARED THAT YOU MIGHT HIT HIM AGAIN.
I DIDN'T KNOW THAT RYAN WAS SCARED.
BUT I'M STILL ANGRY! I DON'T KNOW WHY HE WAS POINTING AND LAUGHING AT ME.
IT SOUNDS LIKE A QUESTION ONLY RYAN CAN ANSWER.
HE ALSO HAS SOME QUESTIONS HE'D LIKE TO ASK YOU. HE'D LIKE TO MEET YOU TO TALK ABOUT WHAT HAPPENED. WOULD YOU LIKE TO MEET HIM?

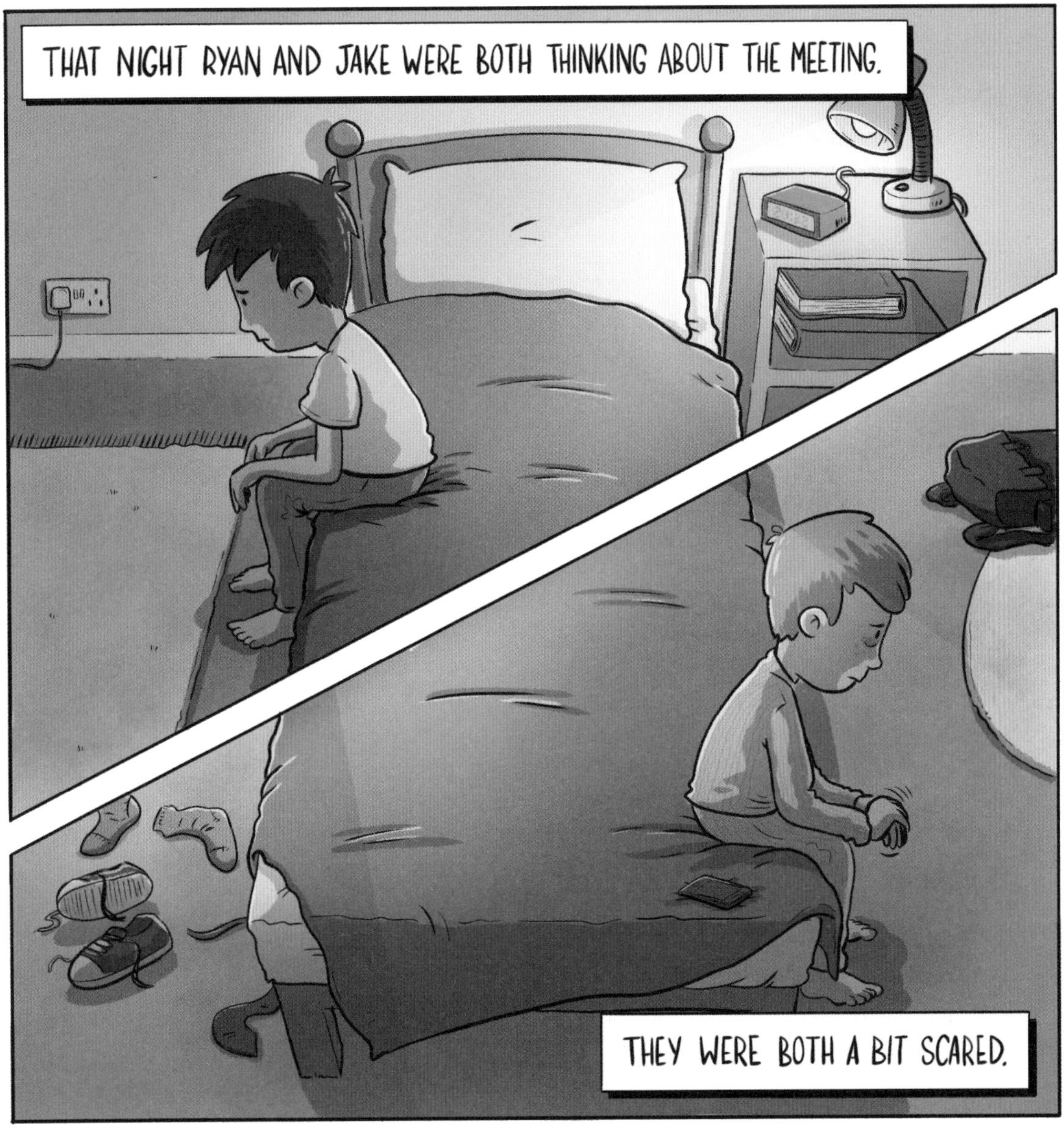
THAT NIGHT RYAN AND JAKE WERE BOTH THINKING ABOUT THE MEETING.
THEY WERE BOTH A BIT SCARED.

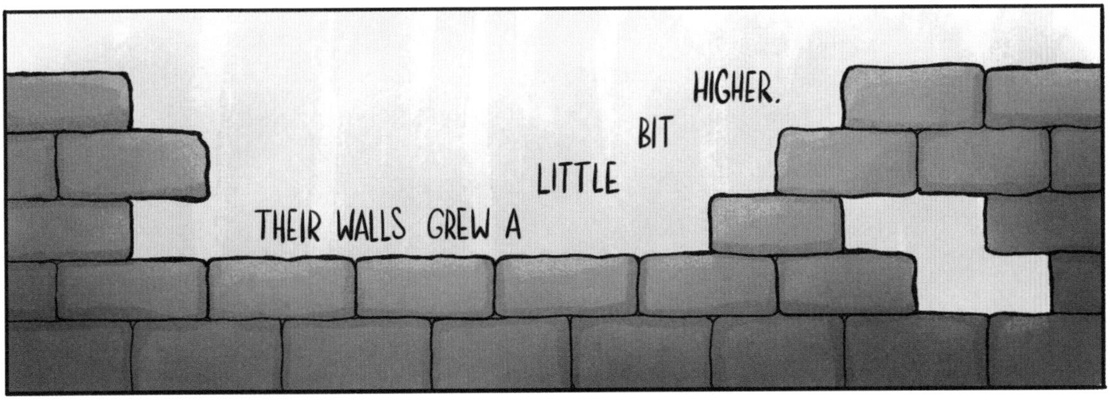
THEIR WALLS GREW A LITTLE BIT HIGHER.

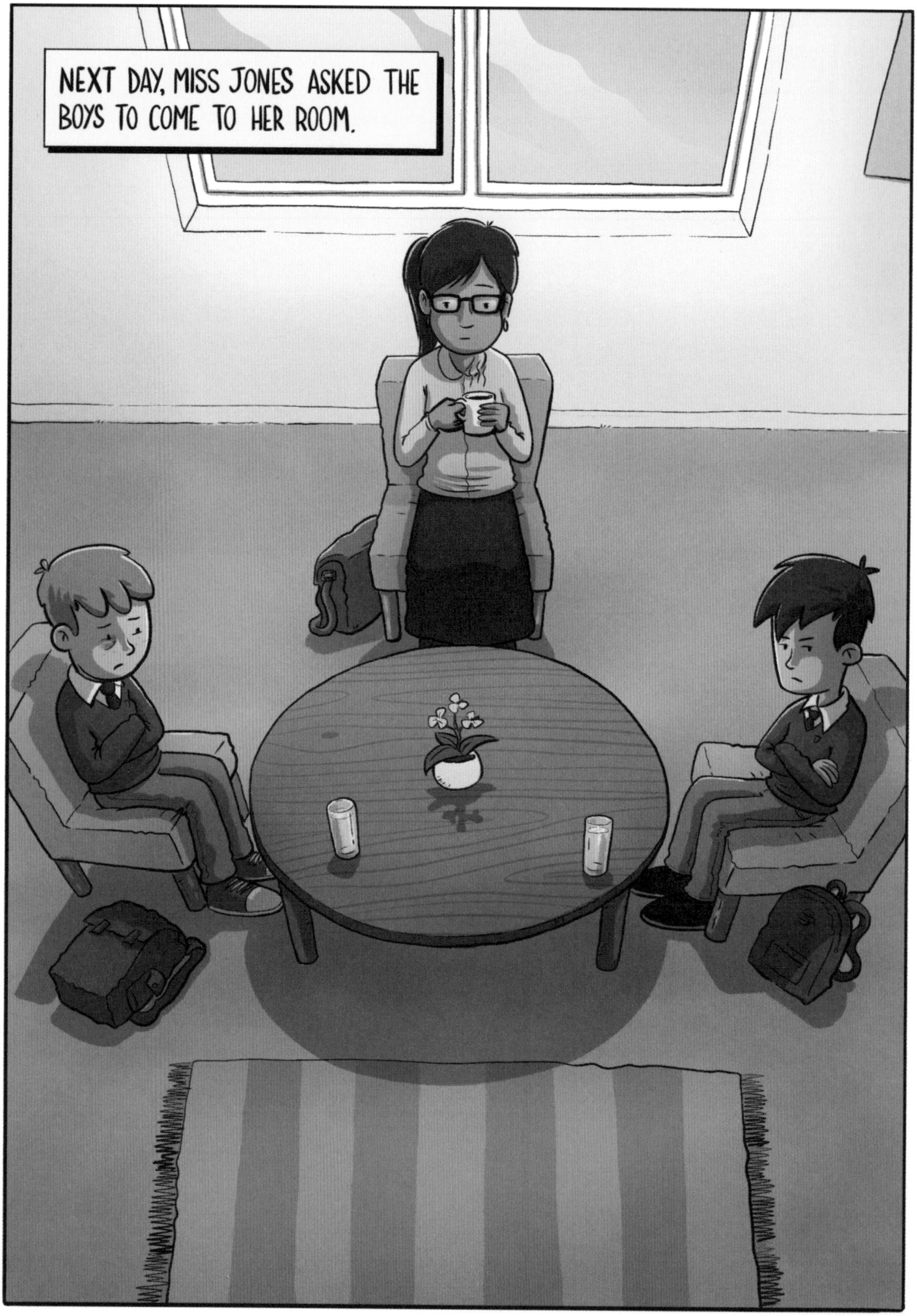
NEXT DAY, MISS JONES ASKED THE BOYS TO COME TO HER ROOM.

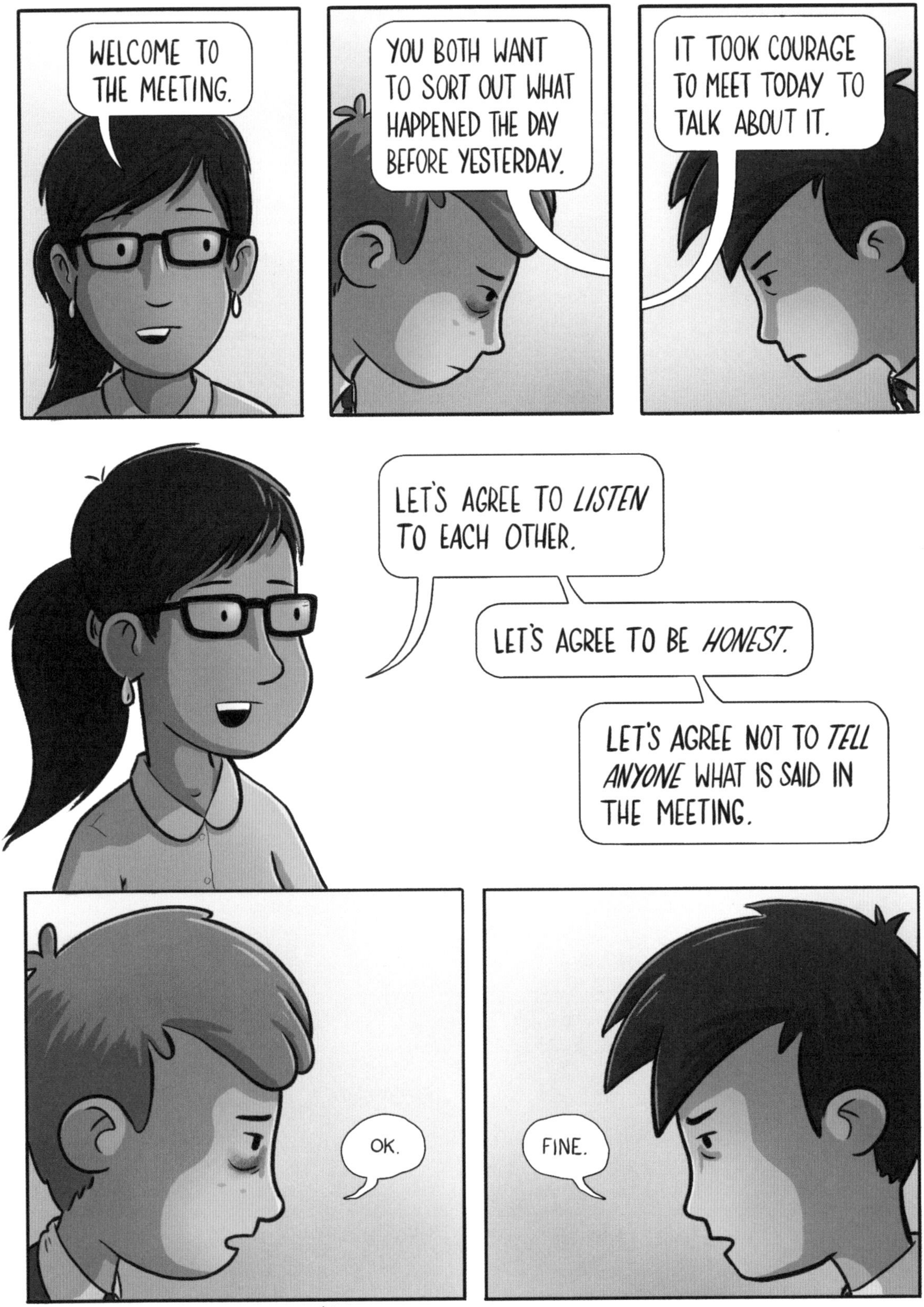
WELCOME TO THE MEETING.
YOU BOTH WANT TO SORT OUT WHAT HAPPENED THE DAY BEFORE YESTERDAY.
IT TOOK COURAGE TO MEET TODAY TO TALK ABOUT IT.
LET'S AGREE TO *LISTEN* TO EACH OTHER.
LET'S AGREE TO BE *HONEST*.
LET'S AGREE NOT TO *TELL ANYONE* WHAT IS SAID IN THE MEETING.
OK.
FINE.

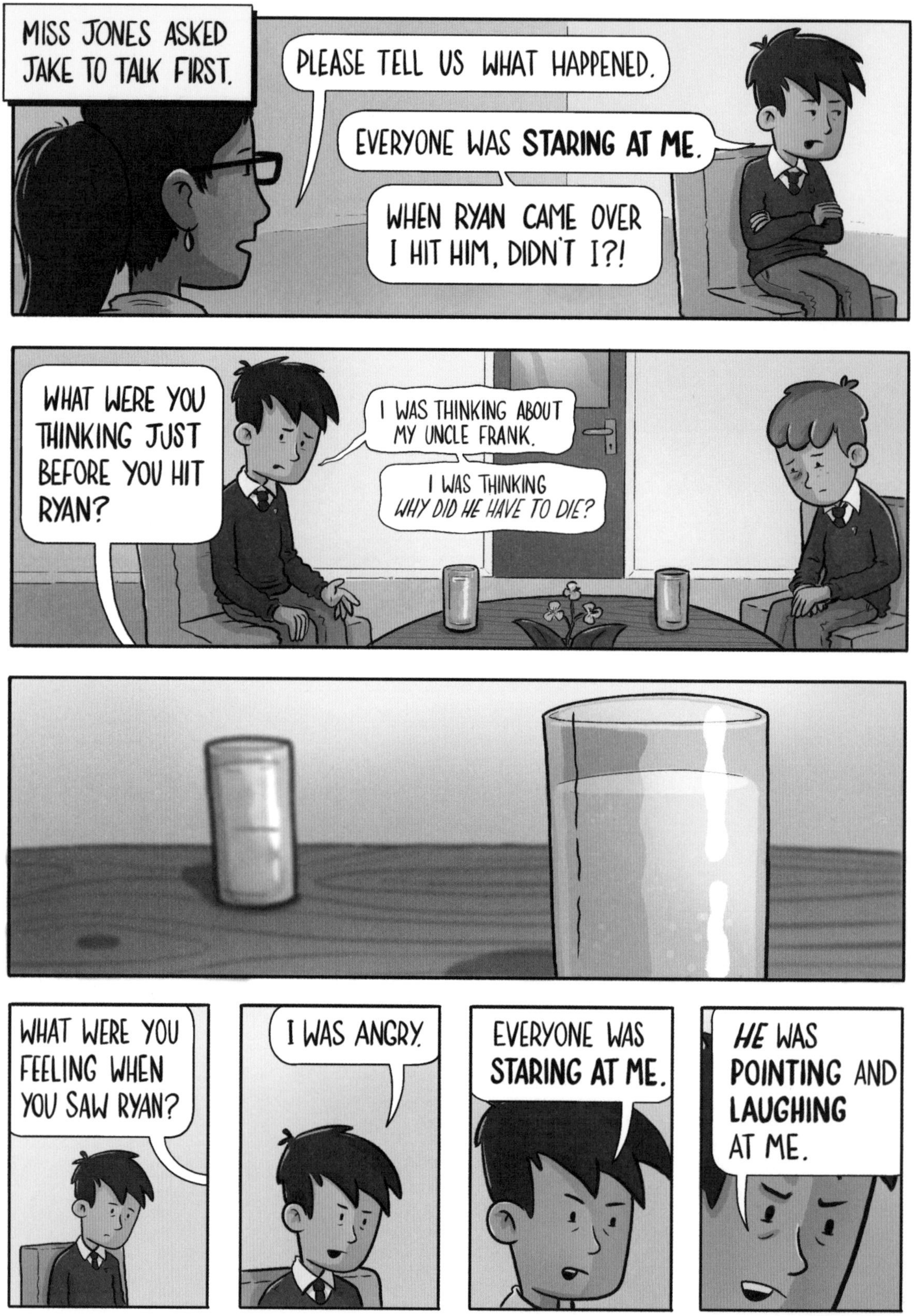

MISS JONES ASKED JAKE TO TALK FIRST.
PLEASE TELL US WHAT HAPPENED.
EVERYONE WAS **STARING AT ME**.
WHEN RYAN CAME OVER I HIT HIM, DIDN'T I?!
WHAT WERE YOU THINKING JUST BEFORE YOU HIT RYAN?
I WAS THINKING ABOUT MY UNCLE FRANK.
I WAS THINKING *WHY DID HE HAVE TO DIE?*
WHAT WERE YOU FEELING WHEN YOU SAW RYAN?
I WAS ANGRY.
EVERYONE WAS **STARING AT ME.**
HE WAS **POINTING** AND **LAUGHING** AT ME.

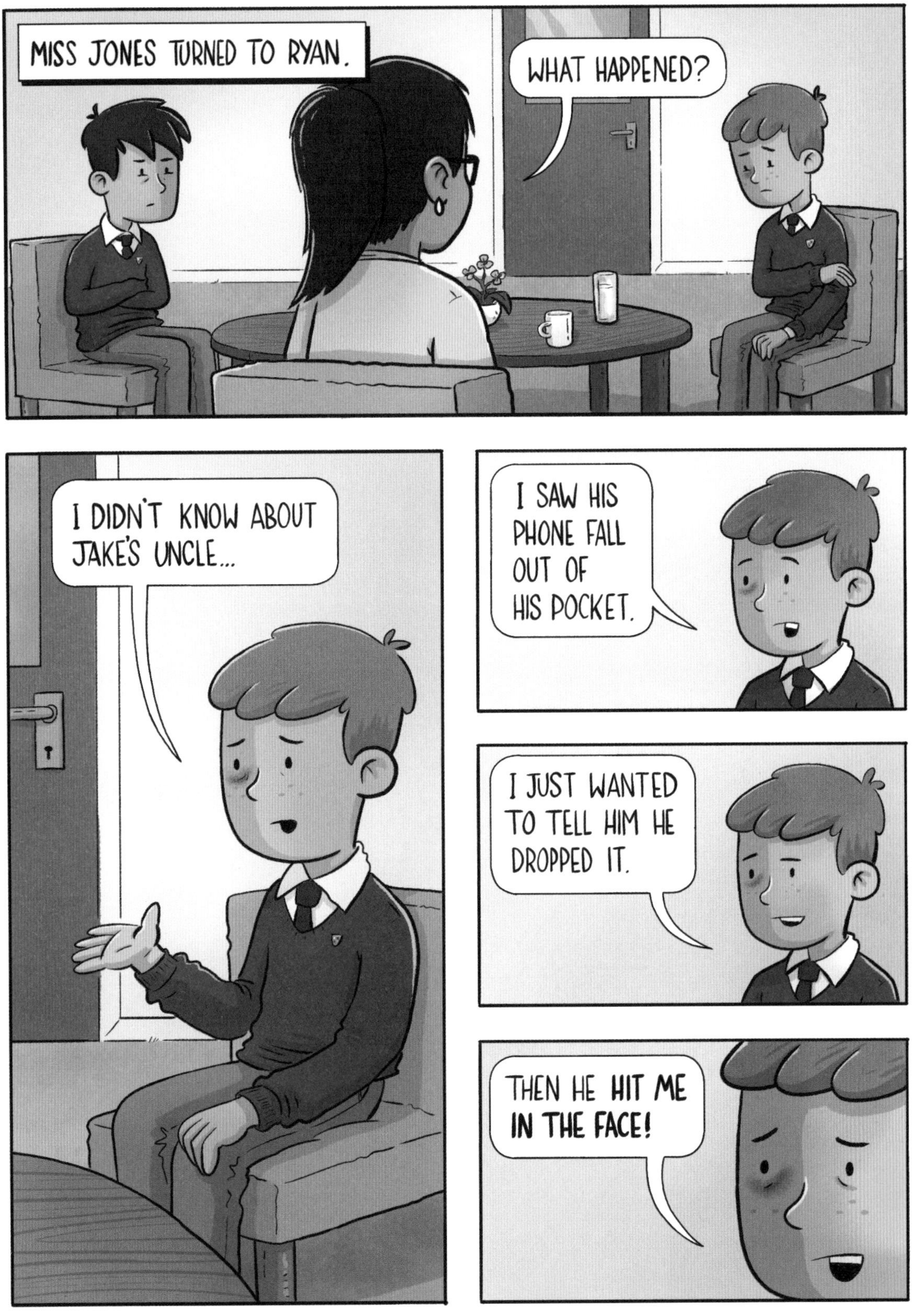
MISS JONES TURNED TO RYAN.
WHAT HAPPENED?
I DIDN'T KNOW ABOUT JAKE'S UNCLE...
I SAW HIS PHONE FALL OUT OF HIS POCKET.
I JUST WANTED TO TELL HIM HE DROPPED IT.
THEN HE **HIT ME IN THE FACE!**

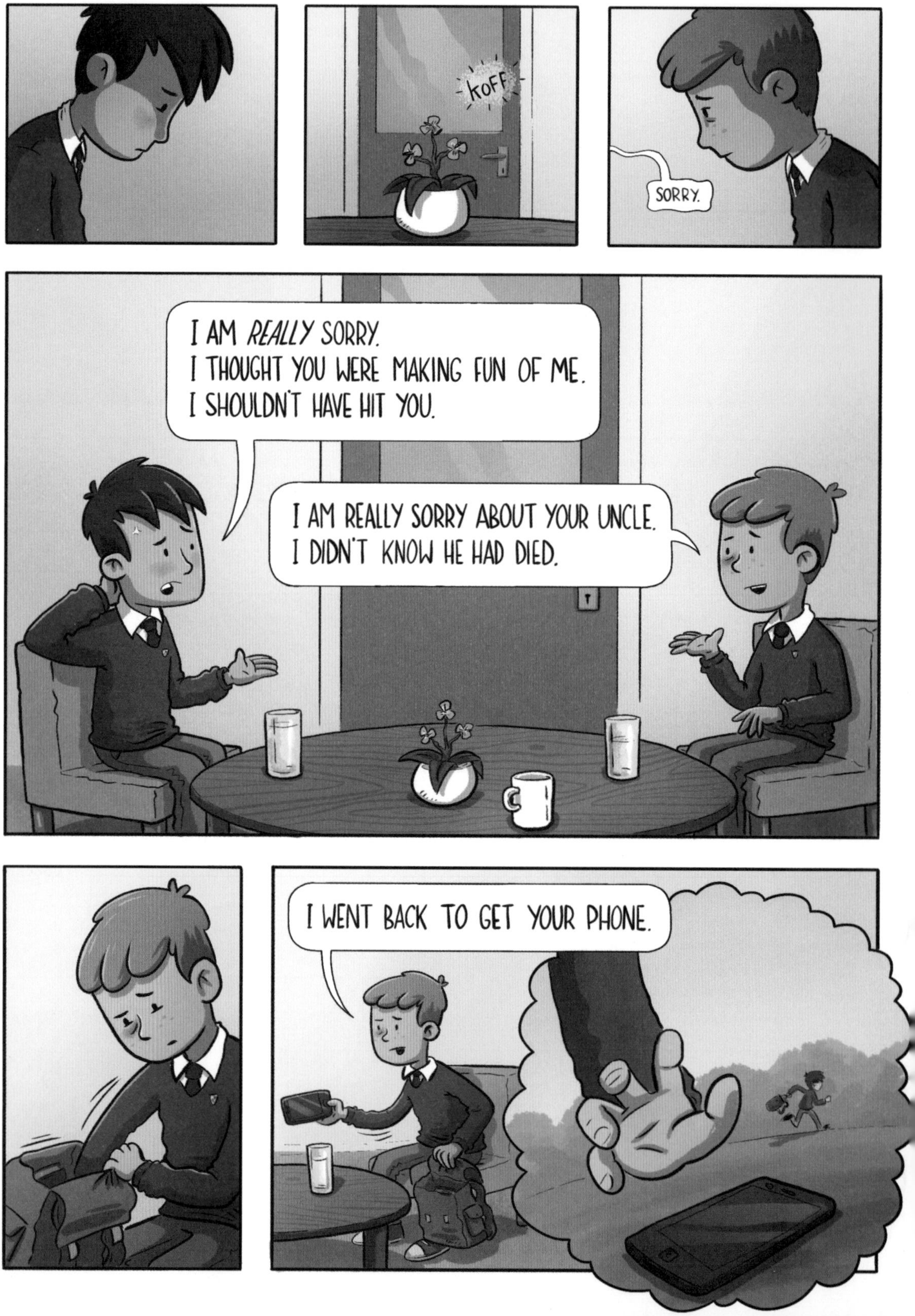
koff
SORRY.
I AM REALLY SORRY.
I THOUGHT YOU WERE MAKING FUN OF ME.
I SHOULDN'T HAVE HIT YOU.
I AM REALLY SORRY ABOUT YOUR UNCLE.
I DIDN'T KNOW HE HAD DIED.
I WENT BACK TO GET YOUR PHONE.

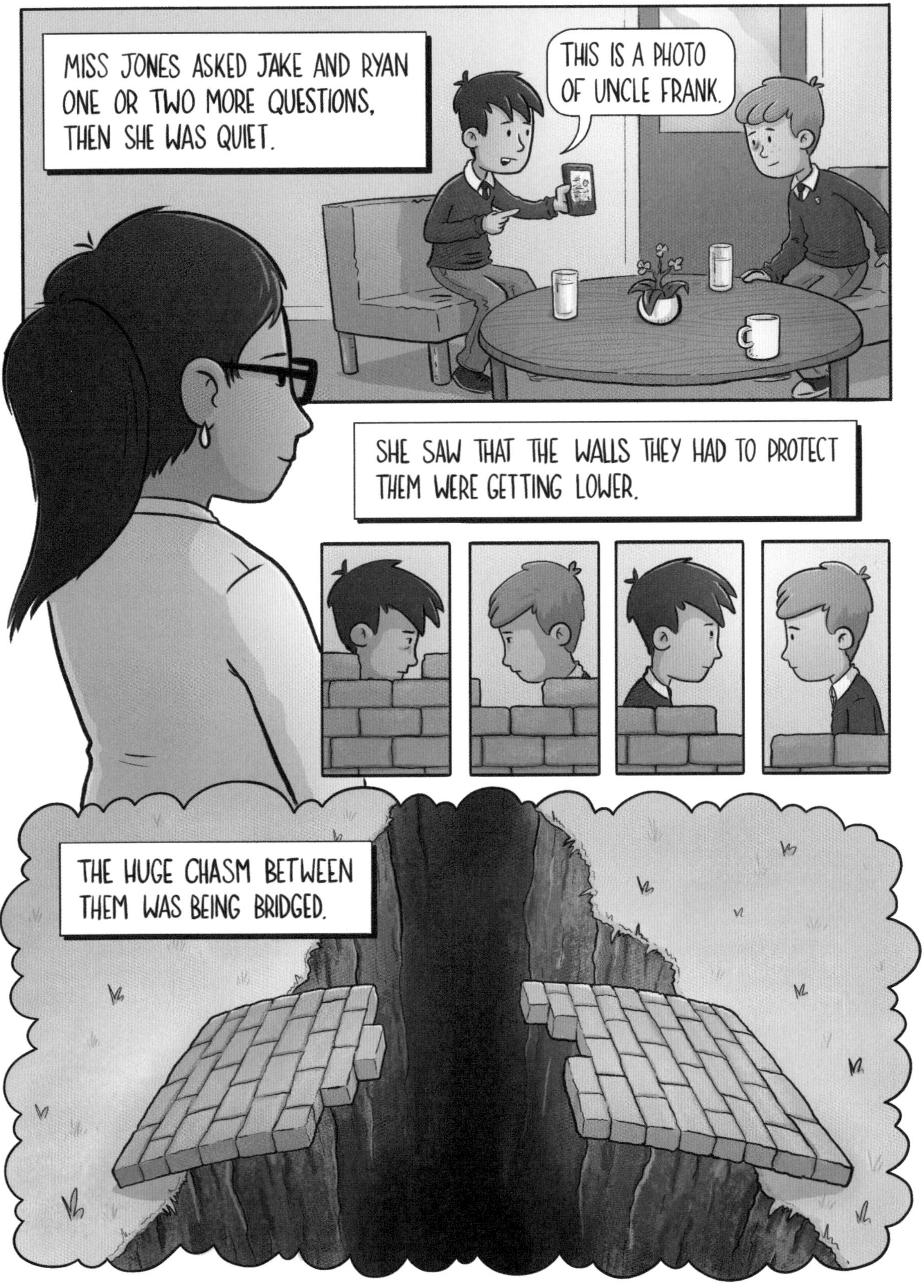
MISS JONES ASKED JAKE AND RYAN ONE OR TWO MORE QUESTIONS, THEN SHE WAS QUIET.
THIS IS A PHOTO OF UNCLE FRANK.
SHE SAW THAT THE WALLS THEY HAD TO PROTECT THEM WERE GETTING LOWER.
THE HUGE CHASM BETWEEN THEM WAS BEING BRIDGED.

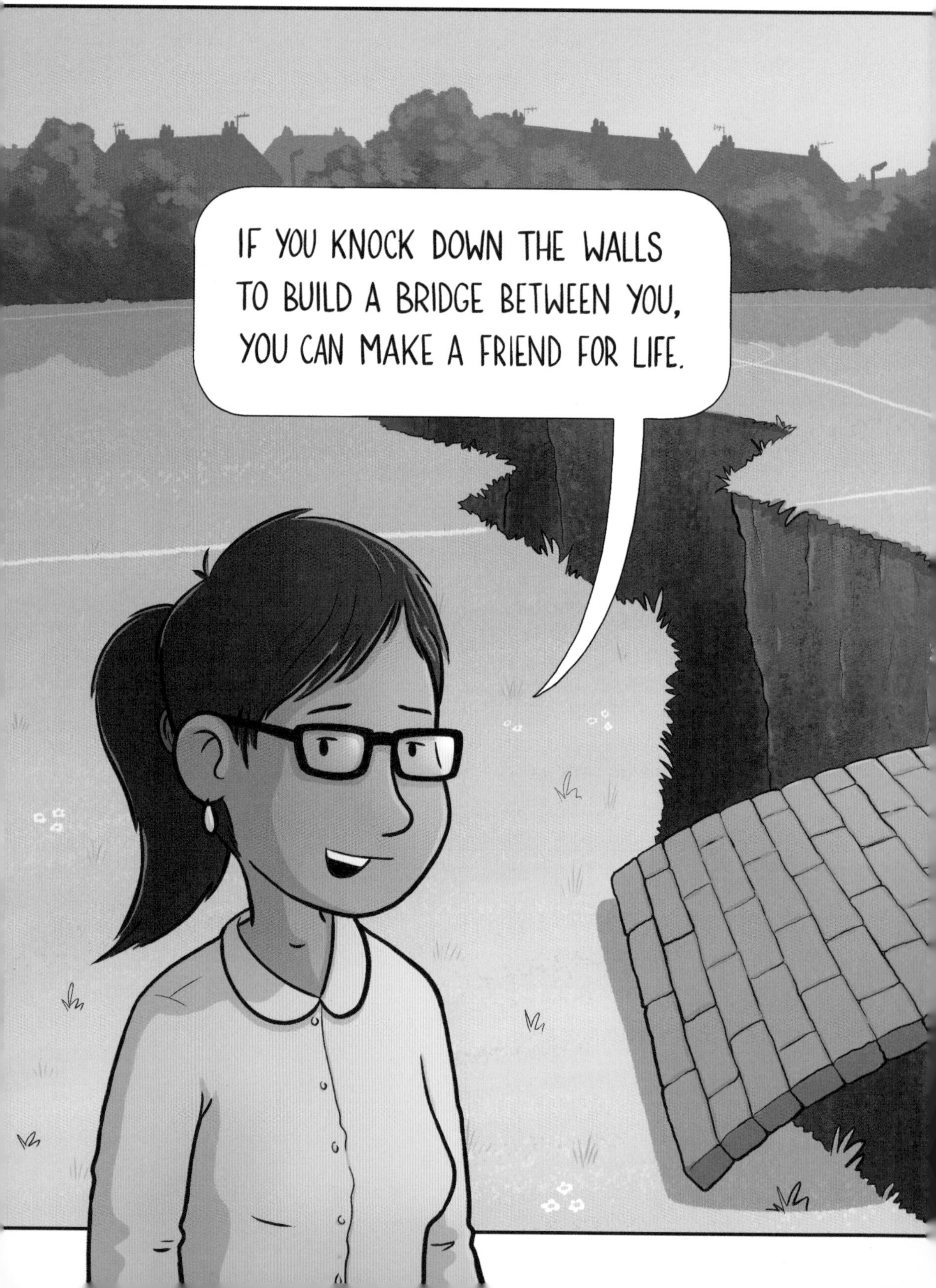
IF YOU KNOCK DOWN THE WALLS TO BUILD A BRIDGE BETWEEN YOU, YOU CAN MAKE A FRIEND FOR LIFE.

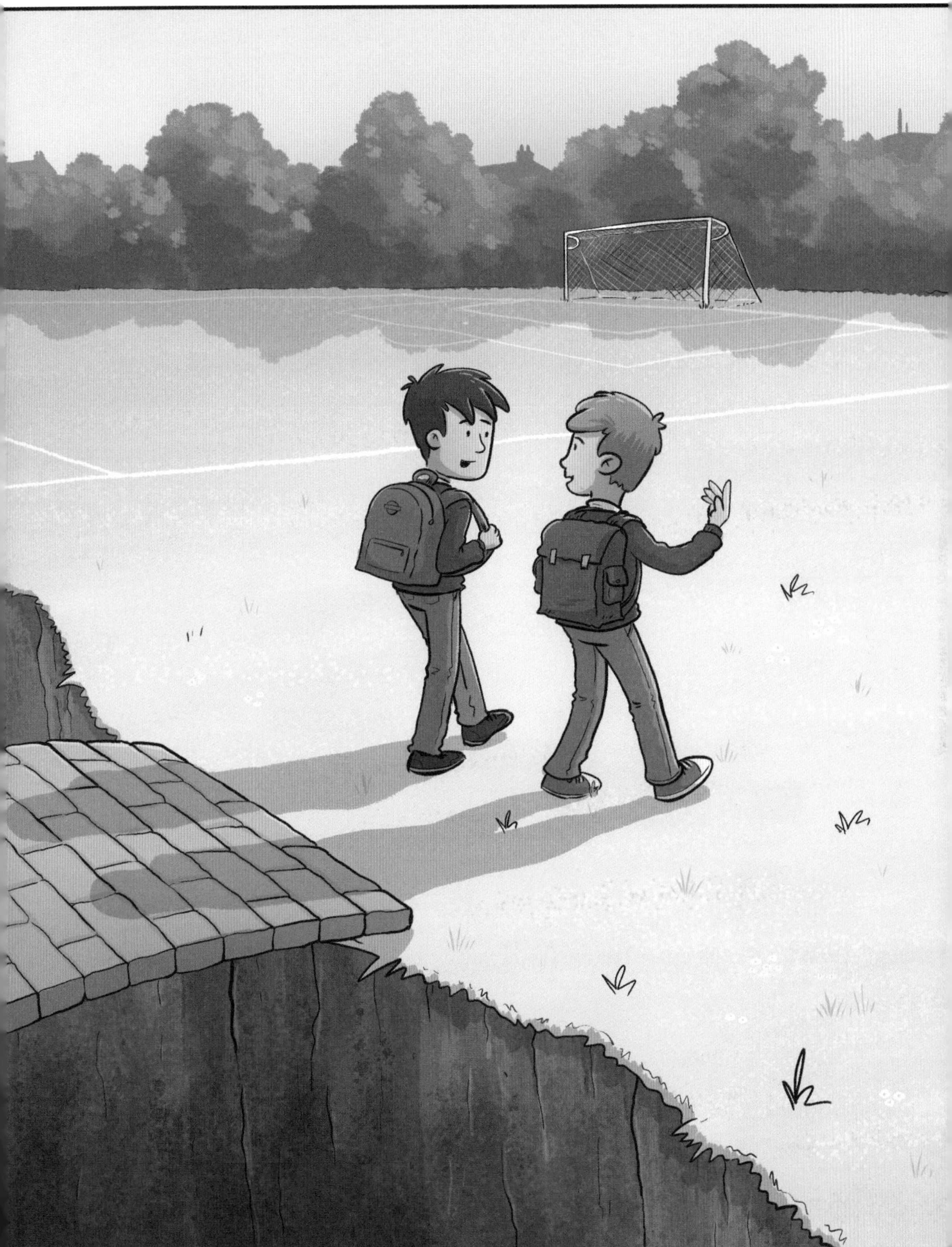

About Restorative Justice

Jake and Ryan are able to sort out their conflict through a restorative justice meeting. Although the term 'restorative justice' may be more familiar from the world of criminal justice, over the past couple of decades people working in a wide range of different contexts have discovered the benefits of the restorative approach. Managing conflict justly is as important in a children's home, school, housing or health setting or neighbourhood as it is following a crime. While some prefer the term 'restorative approaches' to 'restorative justice', people across the globe are finding that restorative values, principles and practices have value in virtually every situation involving relationships between people.

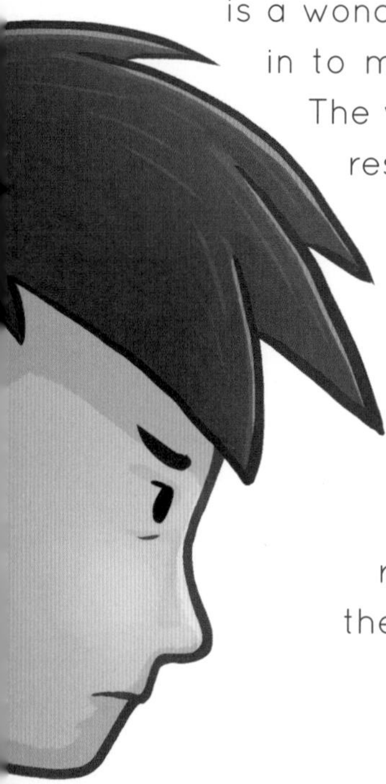

Miss Jones has clearly been trained in restorative justice, but the initial reaction of her school to Jake and Ryan's conflict is both authoritarian and punitive. In a school setting, there is a wonderful opportunity to go beyond simply stepping in to mediate between people when things go wrong. The whole culture and ethos of a school can be made restorative. A restorative school pays attention to the quality of relationships in the classroom, playground and staff room, recognising that putting aside time to nurture relationships leads to a healthier, happier and more productive environment. Restorative justice gives teachers, pupils and parents – indeed, the whole school community – the skills to foster respectful relationships, and to resolve minor conflicts before they escalate.

The five core restorative principles outlined below are the building blocks for creating respectful relationships, and become the steps in the process of repairing relationships when things go wrong:

1. Everyone has a unique perspective
We create time and space for everyone to share their personal stories and narratives through respectful and non-judgemental listening, recognising that good-quality attention is a precious resource.

2. How we behave is connected to our thoughts and feelings
We offer others an insight into our inner world when we talk about our thoughts and feelings. Encouraging emotional literacy helps to tame difficult feelings, and when people share one another's emotional state, empathy develops naturally.

3. Every action has a consequence
We are all connected, and an important part of growing up is to recognise that our every action has consequences for others. If we hurt someone we can learn how others are affected, and by exploring how far the ripples of harm can spread, the restorative approach encourages responsibility and accountability.

4. Needs
Miss Jones asks Jake and Ryan what they need to feel better. When people in a conflict situation are supported in exploring the needs that led to or arise from the conflict, they realise that the only way to meet these needs is through communication with the other person.

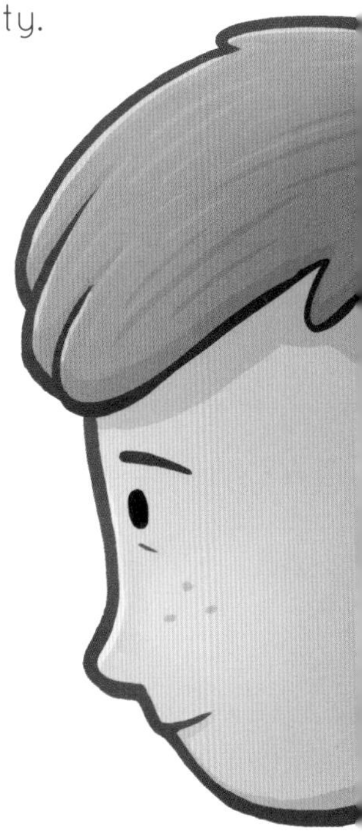

5. The person with the problem is best placed to find the solution
One of the great things about restorative justice is that it releases us from having to fix other people's issues. Once people clearly identify their needs, the way forward naturally follows.

Benefits for schools

Schools that have fully embedded a restorative approach report a reduction in sanctions and exclusions, fewer incidents of violence, criminal damage, racism and aggression, improved academic outcomes and reduced staff sickness. OfSTED recognise the value of restorative justice in creating a positive culture in schools. The approach builds empathy, develops skills in self-management and strengthens the inner moral compass through accountability and empowerment.

Find out more

Belinda Hopkins developed the model based on the five themes or core beliefs described above, drawing on the work of restorative justice pioneers and practitioners from all over the world. Check out her website www.transformingconflict.org and her seminal book *Just Schools* (JKP). The Restorative Justice Council is the national umbrella organisation for restorative justice. Its website provides information about training, resources, quality standards, research and events: www.restorativejustice.org.uk. Written more from a criminal justice perspective, *Understanding Restorative Justice* (Policy Press) provides a clear guide to the inner workings of restorative justice, exploring how the process of bringing people into communication restores connection and develops empathy.

of related interest

Implementing Restorative Practices in Schools
A Practical Guide to Transforming School Communities
Margaret Thorsborne and Peta Blood
ISBN 978 1 84905 377 8
eISBN 978 0 85700 737 7

Cartooning Teen Stories
Using comics to explore key life issues with young people
Jenny Drew
ISBN 978 1 84905 631 1
eISBN 978 1 78450 106 8

How to Create Kind Schools
12 extraordinary projects making schools happier
Jenny Hulme
ISBN 978 1 84905 591 8
eISBN 978 1 78450 157 0

Just Schools
A Whole School Approach to Restorative Justice
Belinda Hopkins
ISBN 978 1 84310 132 1
eISBN 978 1 84642 432 8

A Practical Guide to Restorative Practice for Schools
Theory, Knowledge, Skills and Strategies for Success
Bill Hansberry
ISBN 978 1 84905 707 3
eISBN 978 1 78450 232 4

First published in 2016
by Jessica Kingsley Publishers
73 Collier Street
London N1 9BE, UK
and
400 Market Street, Suite 400
Philadelphia, PA 19106, USA

www.jkp.com

Library of Congress Cataloging in Publication Data
A CIP catalog record for this book is available from the Library of Congress

British Library Cataloguing in Publication Data
A CIP catalogue record for this book is available from the British Library

ISBN 978 1 78592 016 5
eISBN 978 1 78450 260 7

Printed and bound in China

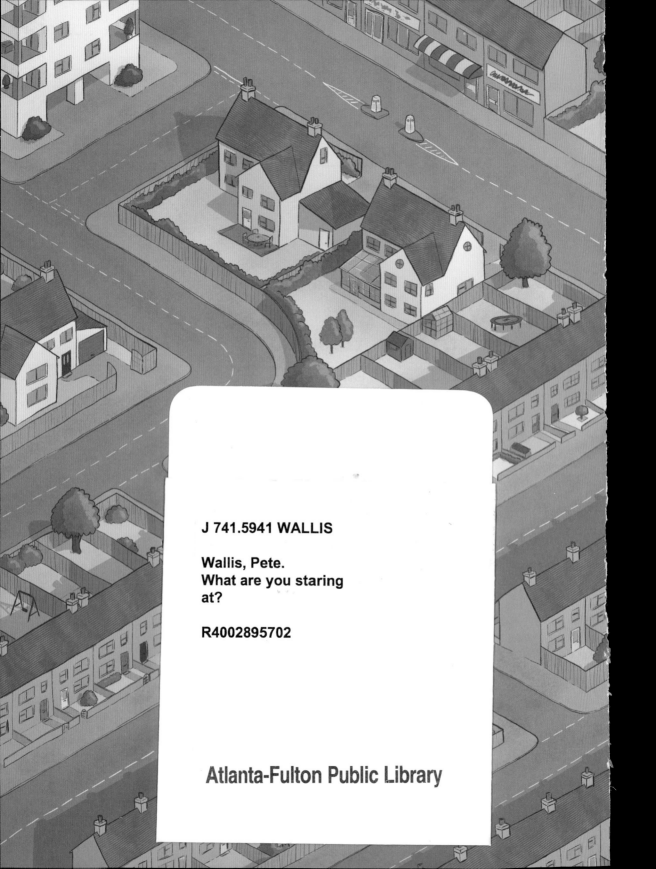